Unlocking Your Credit

Beginner-Friendly Guide To Legally Understand, Repair, And Leverage The Credit System To Your Advantage

Arthur G. Depina

ACKNOWLEDGMENTS

FIRST AND FOREMOST, I WANT to thank God and my wife, Ana Fernandes, for always believing in our mission to help people better their lives through managing and leveraging the power of credit.

Not many spouses would support a new business endeavor or ideas immediately after we had almost lost everything in 2012, and found ourselves out of jobs, lost our house, and with piles of debts and a big family to support. It would have been impossible to solely dedicate myself to learn everything I possibly could about fixing credit, personal finance, opening a business without her unselfish sacrifice. Countless hours were spent (many of them on evenings, sleepless nights, weekends) attempting to pull back the curtain on the hidden secret of the WORLD OF CREDIT.

Thank you most importantly for our beautiful kids, Jada, Jasmin, Joana, AJ, Ava, Kamare, Myles, and Logan. And thank you to my wife's parents Filipe and Maria, for raising a wonderful, Godly, and brilliant woman. I'm blessed to have her in my life!

My generation is standing on the shoulder of a giant, and I am no exception. My single mother, Ernestina Gomes, sacrificed everything to raise me and instilled the non-stop work ethic in my early teenage years and the focus that drives me today. Her generation's ability to break down the barriers in the face of devastating adversity left me with no excuse but to seek greatness, no matter how hard the climbs are. Thank you for believing in me long before anyone else did; I am honored to be your son and most honored to have you as my mother.

And thank you to my two heavenly angels, my father Filipe and brother Emanuel Depina. Finally, thank you to my three beautiful little sisters Amy, Tonisha, and Lisa.

Special thanks to my inner circle of friends and clients that inspired me to share all that I have learned over the years with the world through in-person consultations, social media, Zoom, and seminars.

Too many people helped along the way to achieve this level of success.

INTRODUCTION

Hello, and welcome to the program. I am excited to have you here.

My name is Arthur G. Depina. I am an owner and co-founder of Depina Credit Solutions – a Credit Repair Company located in the metropolitan area of Boston, Massachusetts. Before my wife and I founded this company, my background was in banking, auto, and consumer and business credit.

Today, many people affectionately refer to me as *The Brockton Credit Guy.* This name has been bestowed upon me by the thousands of people in my community (the Brockton area where my business is incorporated) whose lives I have directly influenced positively with my teachings for eight years now.

During this time, I have had much success in reaching people from all walks of life and various parts of the country when I conduct live social media training.

Besides, I regularly create programs meant to teach financial literacy to people at schools, non-profit organizations, banks, businesses, seminars, first-time homebuyer classes, and so on. I also take in clients for one- on– one coaching, where I take them by the hand and help them incorporate the tenets of good credit behavior in their lives.

I have been featured in Yahoo News, Yahoo Finance, as well as Business Insider. Experise.com recently ranked my firm as one of the top 20 credit repair companies for the year 2020.

So, given my extensive background that spans more than a decade long, I would say that I happen to know a thing or two about consumer credit. And I plan to share my knowledge with you in this book.

This book is my gift to you because I realize that in the wake of the recession that we are currently facing - in large part due to Covid-19 – many people have fallen into a financial crisis. The Pew Charitable Trust estimates that 80% of Americans are in debt.

Since you have picked up this book, my guess is, you likely belong in this crowd.

So you need help. And you need it fast. Fair enough.

You see, credit presents a somewhat paradoxical situation. On the one hand, you need it to function well in today's society.

Few people can afford to purchase an automobile, a home, fund college tuition, or meet any number of huge financial obligations by offering cash upfront. The only exception is if you are already wealthy or come from a wealthy household.

So credit serves a very important role in people's lives.

On the other hand, if improperly used, credit can land you into trouble, a lot of trouble. Poor credit can cause problems with seeking employment, qualifying for loans at cheap rates, qualifying for loans at all, getting insurance, gaining entrance to education institutions, fees charged by lenders, and much more.

Bad credit can even cause problems with your significant other. Of all the problems that lead to divorce, few carry as much weight as financial issues, especially indebtedness.

And in case you are not married or in a serious relationship yet, realize that a potential mate who is financially savvy will likely dismiss your involvement with him or her right off the bat if they happen to discover the grave nature of your situation. So yes, bad credit can even cost you, love.

You can't afford to sweep this issue under the rug. So pay attention.

My objective is to show you the ways and means of safely navigating the world of consumer credit – which is forever shrouded in secrecy.

In the chapters to come, we will discuss a wide variety of topics. We will look at what credit is and how a credit score is calculated. We will look at how you can begin building credit in case you don't have one. If your credit is in bad shape, we will look at how you can repair it.

Few people understand that credit reports and credit scores are often inaccurate representations of your financial situation. After all, they are prepared by people who can and often do make mistakes. So, I will devote some time to talking about how you can correct mistakes in credit reports, which will go a long way in improving your credit profile.

We will talk about what a perfect credit profile looks like and the steps you might take to achieve the same result. If your credit is in good shape, we will look at ways to avoid ruining it and getting into trouble.

The lack of financial savvy has led many people to make grievous mistakes when handling situations that involve credit, such as: purchasing your first home, negotiating credit card terms, foreclosures, divorce, repossession, or even bankruptcy.

I will give you some tips and game plans that you can use to navigate such situations without causing much damage to yourself.

Last but not least, we will examine identity theft – arguably one of the most widely perpetrated crimes in the United States – and its serious ramifications on your creditworthiness. We will look at ways you can detect it early enough, how you can report it, and ways of preventing it.

Summed up, this book contains the collective knowledge that will help you get out of trouble and stay out of trouble. It is a distillation of all the useful principles and techniques I have learned throughout the years.

That said, let's get down to business, shall we?

TABLE OF CONTENTS

PART 1:

GETTING A GRIP ON CREDIT

We'll start by getting the fundamentals figured out.

But before we do that, I'll let you in a little bit on what I deal with in the type of work I do.

In the years that I have been involved in advising people and helping them solve their credit problems, I have repeatedly asked several questions.

Here are some of them:

- **What is credit, and what factors go into determining my credit score?**

- **I have no credit history, and banks cannot trust me or even give me any consideration. How do I get started in building a healthy credit without getting into trouble?**

- **I'm just curious how lenders determine the interest they charge me on my car loan, mortgage, credit cards, and so on. And how do I know that it is even fair?**

- **Do bills such as utilities, rent, medical, insurance, and so on affect my credit?**

- **The credit scores I see on reports generated by monitoring services such as credit karma and credit sesame seem a lot different from those the banks use when evaluating me for a loan. Why is that so? Is there anything I can do about it?**

- **What constitutes a good, bad, or great credit score?**

- **Why do I have such a poor credit score, yet I earn a decent income and pay my bills on time?**

These are, without doubt, important questions. And ones that most of us are dying to get answers to. I will seek to answer each one of them, and more, such that by the time you are done, you won't have any doubt in your mind regarding how to handle your credit matters.

What Is Credit?

You've seen and heard me use the word **CREDIT** several times now. But what does it mean exactly?

Webster's Dictionary defines credit as the ability to obtain goods or services now, with the expectation that payment will be made at a future date.

And that's what it boils down to. Credit is all about spending tomorrow's cash today.

Let's say it is the weekend all over again (God, I love weekends!). It has been a long week at work, and you've decided to just chill out at the mall. So off you go.

You have no plans to buy anything since it's mid of the month and your wallet is all dried-up. Your business today is *"just looking."*

As you window-shop, you decide to step into a designer clothes store. Why did you even decide to step into such an exclusive store? Because the huge *50% off on all products* sign was hard to miss.

Upon entry, your eye gets drawn towards a bespoke grey suit on the right – the real thing. You've always loved designer suits, but they've always been out of your price range. Your boss happens to own a couple of them, and they always look nice on him.

You hope to own one, especially since there are rumors that you will be promoted to CFO next month.

You stand there, drooling. The suit looks amazing. And so does its price – a cool $3,000. The salesman spots your interest and almost trips over himself to get to you.

He announces to you that today, you can have it at $1500 – a steal. You know it's true. But you politely turn him down, informing him that $1500 is a touch too much for now. He whispers into your ear, "If you have a good line of credit, you could have it right now!"

Now, this is a *once-in-a-lifetime* kind of deal. So, you enthusiastically walk with him over to the counter. You sign a bunch of papers and hand over your credit card. When it's all said and done, you walk away with your dream suit, excited to surprise your colleagues on Monday.

The scenario above plays out over and over again in the lives of people. It's a classic use of credit. Sometimes we use it to acquire luxuries. Other times we use it to acquire or pay for more important things.

Credit is essential in today's way of life. Few people can get by without using it.

Think about it this way: how many people do you happen to know who can afford to pay cash for their home? Note that the median price of homes in the U.S is currently reported to be $226,800.

And what about cars? What of home furniture? What of college tuition?

Before you rush to jump to your conclusions, keep in mind that an interesting survey was conducted in 2019, showing that most Americans live paycheck-to-paycheck. According to the study titled, **"Most Americans lack Savings,"** 70% of Americans have less than $1,000 stashed away in savings.

Such an abysmal savings rate should bring home an important point – most people simply don't have the means to pay for everything in cash.

This is perhaps why the credit industry thrives the way it does. Consumer debt is at an all-time high. Consider the following facts, which were derived from a study conducted by Experian in March 2020.

- Mortgage debt stands at $9.6 trillion.

- Auto loans stand at $1.3 trillion.

- Student loans stand at $1.4 trillion.

- Credit card debt is at $829 billion outstanding.

- Home Equity Lines Of Credit (HELOC) balances stand at $420 billion

- Personal debt is at $305 billion

- Retail credit card debt $90 billion

These are mind-boggling numbers. This is perhaps why America's biggest banks, such as Capital One, Citi, Wells Fargo, Bank of America, and JP Morgan Chase, are in the lending business. Americans borrow.

Okay, the next thing you need to understand about credit is that it is based on trust. Are you an honorable person? Do you stay true to your commitments? Have you worked hard enough to be worthy of trust?

While lending may be such a profitable business, it is important to keep in mind that it is not risk-free. There is always the possibility that a borrower will default on their debt. When that happens, the lender loses.

And that is where the issue of bad credit comes in. In the lending business, you are judged according to your past behavior.

If you have a bad history of using credit (or have no history at all), then you are a risky proposition in the eyes of a lender. And that can be a really bad thing unless you wake up and get things under control.

What You Don't Know Might Hurt You - What Bad Credit Can Do To You

What risk are you running when your credit is in bad shape?

People often make the mistake of underestimating the consequences of bad credit. Since most people are in debt, you may fall for a false sense of security. You reason that you are not alone in this, after all.

Make no mistake about it. I have had the privilege of meeting people from all walks of life who are burdened with credit problems. I have witnessed the negative effects. The most common ones include:

1. *High fees*

The first problem you will face with bad credit has to do with fees.

Whenever you fall behind on your debt payments, you place yourself at risk. This is because late payments are reported by your lender (or lenders), and these show up on your credit report. Consequently, your credit score goes down as a result.

When your credit score goes down, you are inviting trouble. Lenders will perceive you as a high-risk borrower. This opens the door for them to slap high fees. They compensate themselves for the extra risk they are taking in doing business with you in their minds.

The most common fees out there among lenders include:

- **Penalty fees**

- **Late fees**

- **Default rates**

- **Over-limit fees**

- **Repo fees**

- **Legal fees**

- **Deficiency payments**

Now, you need to understand something basic – banks and other lenders love fees. Their entire business model thrives around it.

So, in the pursuit of enormous profit, your lender will not hesitate to charge you a fee whenever they get the chance. Banks love customers who are in a somewhat tight spot credit-wise. They lust after people who can afford only to make minimum payments on cards or other forms of credit. In the industry, these people have a name – revolvers.

These are the ideal customers because penalties and late fees can be added to their balances. And as long as they can retain you, it's pretty good business for them.

It is typical for revolvers to pay more in fees than the amount owed over a loan's life. In the meantime, the interest plus balance on your account continues to mount.

This is how you end up in a situation where you owe more on your card than you had ever envisioned. It's usually a matter of taking you for a ride and dumping you before you do much damage to them.

2. *High-interest rates*

Another painful consequence of having bad credit is that you get charged more interest.

Remember, lenders are always looking to offset their risk of lending to a borrower with less-than-stellar credit. The burden of high interest becomes even more apparent when considering a huge loan such as an auto loan or a mortgage.

To illustrate what I mean here, imagine two people with different credit scores heading to a lender to apply for a $300,000 mortgage. One of them has a score of 750. The other has a score of 620.

Now, the one with the higher score may get the mortgage at an interest rate of 3.2%. The one with the lower score may get the same amount at 4.8%.

Not too bad, is it? After all, a 1.6% difference shouldn't make much of a difference or even raise eyebrows, right? Wrong!

Let's say that the term on the mortgage was 30 years. That means, over the life of the loan, the one with the higher interest rate pays $99,000 more. That's almost $100,000.

How would you feel about having to pay such a heavy amount? $100,000 isn't chump change.

And so it is with other types of debts. If the impact is that bad with long-term secured credit with lower interest, it is certainly a lot worse with short-term unsecured credit, which usually carries more interest.

The main reason why this problem often goes undetected is that most people never pay attention to the numbers.

3. *Few borrowing options*

We've talked about how credit is almost essential to most people's lives. When your credit is bad and money is tight in the economy, you will have difficulty getting lenders to give you any money.

Most reputable lenders have very high standards regarding who they choose to do business with. If your credit is poor, you may only be eligible for sub-prime loans (expensive loans with strict terms) at best or no loans at all.

Consider this fact: most reputable lenders such as Citi, Wells Fargo, HSBC, and so on, require borrowers to have good to excellent credit scores. By this, I mean credit scores of at least 670 (for FICO) or 700 (for Vantage).

Getting a loan for your mortgage may be a bit more convenient since most lenders will require a FICO score of at least 620.

Special programs such as FHA offered will require a lower score of at least 500, but the terms will stipulate mandatory mortgage insurance plus a 10% down-payment. Thus, your overall costs of obtaining a loan go up.

If your credit is a lot worse, then the lenders will not touch your business with a ten-foot pole.

And when your options are narrowed down in this manner, you are only left with loan sharks such as issuers of payday loans, pawnbrokers, and title loan providers.

These are predatory lenders who will eat you alive and make your life a total misery.

4. *Trouble with renting*

If you think that the issue of credit only affects you if you plan on being a homeowner, think again.

It turns out that most landlords and property management companies are concerned about tenants who have poor credit.

Landlords reasonably assume that the way you handle your debt obligations reflects how you will handle rent payments.

Just think about it; how would you like to be a landlord (or landlady) with a tenant who is not likely to pay on time? One who is likely to be months in arrears?

It's not a good position to be in, is it? You probably service a mortgage payment, especially because you financed the purchase or construction of the building. The last thing you want is trouble with your Lender.

Therefore, one of the few things landlords want is trouble with rent payments. So, you can expect that they will ask to check your credit as part of the vetting process.

Experian did a study that showed that 620 is typically the minimum score that will guarantee you little or no trouble renting an apartment.

Anything less than that means that you will probably have to jump through hoops while trying to acquire a nice place to rent. In some instances, you will have to part with a hefty security deposit or get a cosigner.

5. *Few employment opportunities*

It's also worth noting that not many employers are enthusiastic about hiring someone who has credit problems.

A 2016 poll by CareerBuilder established that more than seven out of every ten employers run a credit check for any new hire. And three out of ten reported using credit checks as part of the process of evaluating on-the-job performance.

Now, you would think that creditworthiness is the last thing that would be on an employer's mind, especially because they are the ones who pay you and not the other way round.

But the fact is, there is a significant correlation between job performance and financial health. Many employers reason that credit problems are likely to serve as distractions that lead to handling work responsibly.

Another line of reasoning is that credit problems are an indicator of responsibility. So, most employers feel that a failure to handle debt obligations is a probable indicator of problems with important assignments.

Lastly, bad credit, in a way, depicts your level of trustworthiness. So, most employers would think twice about hiring someone with a bad credit history or going bankrupt for a top-level position or a job that involves financial transactions.

6. *Higher premiums on insurance*

There's something else that you might overlook regarding the issue of poor credit- the likelihood of paying high premiums on auto insurance.

Actuaries at insurance companies have established a significant positive relationship between accident insurance claims and lower credit scores.

So, insurance companies are under the impression that people with credit problems are likely to get involved in accidents and subsequently file for claims.

On the face of it, the whole idea makes total sense. If you are overburdened with credit, you are less likely to pay attention to safe driving on the road since your mind will be filled with troubled thoughts.

This means added risk to the insurer. Therefore, people with bad credit are likely to pay higher premiums or be dropped from consideration altogether. The Zebra did a report that revealed that car owners with poor credit scores were likely to pay more than twice the insurance premium paid by those with excellent scores.

Providers of renters' and homeowner's insurance are also likely to charge you higher premiums based on this merit alone. Life insurers are also likely to drag their feet in issuing you with a policy when it is clear to them that you have serious credit problems as well.

7. *Divorce*

Few things have the power to sever the connection between you and your significant other quite in the way that financial issues do.

It is often reported that more than 50% of marriages end in divorce. And in most cases, financial matters are the leading cause of such disputes.

Imagine this scenario and see if you don't agree with me that it is unromantic. You go out shopping with your family on the weekend, and you load up the cart with tons of items.

Later, with your sweetheart standing next to you at the checkout, you pull out your credit card.

Upon swiping, the woman serving you informs you that your card has been declined. You inform her that it must be a mistake and urge her to try once again. She accepts your request. Again, the beeping sound.

You reach into your wallet and pull out the Discover Platinum Card. You urge her to try that one instead. She complies. Again, the same thing happens.

Now, everyone waiting in line is witnessing whatever is happening. You can even hear some snickering at the back. You break into a cold, clammy sweat. You politely urge the cashier to take out a few items. She swipes the card again—the same problem.

At this point, you are not only deeply embarrassed; you are exasperated. You help her unload half the items on your cart before the transaction goes through.

You leave the store taking care not to lock eyes with anybody in sight.

Can you imagine a more humiliating experience? Without a doubt, you likely can't.

This and many similar issues have the power to drive even the most devoted partners apart. So, be sure that your finances are in proper shape before your love is put to the ultimate test.

Now that we've seen the unimaginable consequences of bad credit let's move up and look at how you can assess your financial situation to determine the likelihood of credit problems.

Determining Your Financial Health

Fixing credit problems requires that you get the overall picture of your financial situation.

In other words, it calls for determining your financial health. Once you determine how good or bad your financial health is, you can begin to take corrective steps.

Knowing your net worth

One of the best ways to determine your financial health that exist out there is by establishing your net worth.

Not many people can accurately reveal what their net worth is. I am particularly not in favor of the celebrity net worth figures published online by some more popular websites. Often, these figures are misrepresented.

A case in point involves the famed RnB star, Robert Kelly. Before he was indicted, his net worth was reported to be at $200 million. Then during the proceedings, it turned out that he hadn't paid child support and couldn't come up with $100,000 to bail himself out. Soon, it became clear that the man was close to bankruptcy.

You see, people tend to use erroneous information to calculate net worth. Often, this leads people to overestimate how much they (or other people) are worth, financially speaking.

This section will let you in on the real scoop of how net worth is calculated. Granted, we may leave some items out, but it is better to underestimate your financial position than to overestimate it.

Let's begin with the definition of net worth.

So, what is net worth exactly?

Simply, net worth is a statement of your financial position, determined by the difference between your assets and your liabilities.

Now, your assets represent all the cash you have at your disposal, plus everything else you own that has monetary value, and that has a ready market - meaning, your assets can be readily exchanged for cash.

Your savings, for instance, fall under the category of assets. The same goes for real estate holdings, retirement and pension plans, business income, stocks, bonds, precious metals, Certificates of Deposits (CDs), money market accounts, and much more.

This reminds me of an issue I need to address at this point. Many people will advise you to include consumer artifacts such as cars, clothing, furniture, and related items in the assets column. Bankers may certainly do this.

I highly advise against it because such a practice often leads to a false estimation of one's net worth.

Here's why. An item qualifies to be called an asset only if it tends to hold its value or appreciates. The same cannot be said for most consumer artifacts. They tend to depreciate.

Let me ask you this - exactly how much do you think the 50-inch curved TV you bought last year is worth today? What are the odds that you will sell it at the same price you bought it or even a higher one? How about your car.

You know the answer.

The fact is, most of the things we acquire, thinking that they are assets, aren't. They are liabilities.

Perhaps Robert Kiyosaki put it best when he said, *"An asset is something that puts money in your pockets. A liability takes money out of your pockets."*

In financial terms, though, liabilities represent every debt obligation that you have. This is where items such as mortgages, auto loans, credit card balances, payday loans, loans from friends and relatives, student loans, and so forth belong.

That said, your task at this point is to do a tally of all your assets and liabilities. And once you can find the difference in both totals, you will have a good idea of your net worth.

The table below should give you an idea of what I mean.

Assets		Liabilities	
Real Estate holdings	$50,000	Credit Cards	$10,000
Pension fund	$400,000	Mortgage	$100,000
Stocks	$100,000	Student loan	$50,000
Home value	$300,000	Auto loan	$20,000
Savings	$10,000		
Total	**$860,000**	**Total**	**$180,000**

What you are looking at is a simplified version of a balance sheet. A balance sheet is often used in the business world to determine the financial position of a business. The formula is the same. Determine all the assets as well as the liabilities in the enterprise and find the difference.

In our case, the difference between the two columns is $680,000. So the person in the hypothetical scenario above is doing well financially. If a business had the same figures as the one above, it would be declared solvent.

Now, if the figure came up negative, it would be an indication of a problem. A business with a negative difference in its balance sheet would be described as bankrupt or in trouble.

And that is the situation many people find themselves in today. Even among high-income earners, there aren't too many people who have the kind of net worth depicted in the above scenario.

Most people either have lower levels of net worth or are in debt. Negative net worth is a sign that you have too much debt.

If that's the situation you find yourself in, don't despair or beat yourself up. Just realize that you now are in a position to start taking steps in the right direction.

Your Debt To Income Ratio

There is yet another way to measure your financial health. It is by determining what is known as your debt to income ratio (DTI).

Your debt to income ratio is a figure that measures your monthly use of credit. Lenders often use it as one of the ways of measuring your debt load to determine how risky of a proposition you are.

It is a great way to measure your financial health as well. A high DTI ratio should indicate trouble that needs the steps that we will go through in the rest of the book.

So, to determine your DTI ratio, you use the following formula:

DTI ratio = <u>Total Monthly Debt Obligations</u> X 100%

Gross Monthly Income

Based on the formula above, your steps should be as follows:

1. First, tally up all your monthly debt payments.

2. Second, add up all your monthly income before tax.

3. Divide the two and multiply the result by 100%

Now, what good is the number you come up with?

There is a general rule of thumb that you should keep in mind: The lower the number, the better off you are. The converse is also true.

But, just to be on the safe side, stick to the following guidelines.

- **36% or less:** You are carrying a healthy amount of debt load. You shouldn't be looking to add to it if you want to remain valuable in the eyes of creditors.

- **37% - 42%:** Not bad. But you could do better. Seek ways to start minimizing your debt if your score falls under this category.

- **43% - 49%:** You are in trouble. You should be looking for aggressive means of paring down your debts.

- **50% or more:** You are in serious trouble and should be seeking professional assistance.

READING AND UNDERSTANDING YOUR CREDIT REPORT

At this point, you are starting to get a clearer picture of your financial situation. We'll improve on that picture by adding yet another element to the mix – your credit report.

What Is A Credit Report?

Simply put, a credit report is a document that summarizes your borrowing history.

Like I said before, **lenders or individuals that review your report** judge you from your past. It is the only way they can predict your future behavior and reliability when paying back their money. A credit report helps them do that quickly and concisely.

The information in a credit report is assembled from a variety of sources, including but not limited to:

- Banks

- Credit card companies

- Governments

- Public records

- Collection agencies

- Insurance companies

- Landlords

- Utility companies

- Retailers

Companies that are involved in the business of collecting borrower information and creating credit reports are called credit reporting agencies "CRA." Other names are credit bureaus or consumer reporting agencies.

That said, there are three main credit reporting agencies in the United States. They are **Experian, Equifax, and Transunion**. We'll be examining them in greater detail later on.

How Do You Get Access To Your Credit Report?

You need to know how you can access your credit report whenever you need it.

An important thing to note is that the law (Federal Fair Credit Reporting Act) requires that the three main credit bureaus must issue a free credit report, once every year, to all Americans. This report is issued upon request.

The rest of the time, you will be required to pay for access to your credit report.

That said, there are three ways to access your credit report. The first is via the web. The second is by placing a phone call. The third is by placing a request via the mail.

I recommend the first approach. With the flexibility of today's modern technology, I see little reason to go through the trouble associated with the remaining two.

There is also a web portal put together by these three main agencies – simply visit www.annualcreditreport. com. Navigating the website is pretty self-explanatory. You can enlist the help of a tech-savvy relative or friend if you are having problems.

You can also place a phone call to 877 322 8228 and give instructions on how you expect to receive your credit report.

Lastly, you can download a form from the **Federal Trade Commission** website and mail it to this address:

Annual credit Report Request Service

P.O. Box 105281

Atlanta, GA 30348 – 5281

How To Read Your Credit Report

If you are like most people, the first look at a credit report can be intimidating. There is too much information, and you can't seem to make any sense of it.

It's like walking into a pilot's cockpit for the first time and seeing all the various controls and gauges. For the untrained mind, the sight is completely horrifying.

But after you have been taught what every piece of that technology means, the fear departs.

It's the same thing with a credit report. With a little insight, understanding the information in credit reports is not an arduous task.

Sample credit report

For illustration purposes, we will use the sample credit report below.

Granted, the information in it is overly summarized. I've intentionally done so for the benefit of your comprehension. Most real-world credit reports are more detailed than the sample shown.

Another thing - this is just but a standard template.

The reality is, the three credit bureaus all have unique formatting for their reports.

But, despite the formatting's uniqueness, all credit reports contain the same categories of information. Understanding those information categories is the goal of this section.

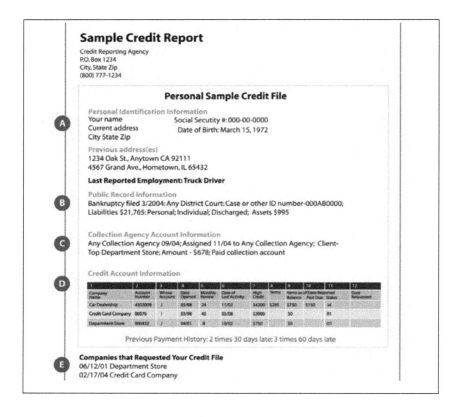

Information category 1: Personal Data

Usually, the first section of every credit report will contain personal information.

Much of the time, the data points include:

- Your Social Security Number (SSN)

- Your cellphone number

- Your address (both past and present)

- Employment status (including your employer name, industry, the position held, length of time spent in employment, and salary)

A more expanded version of this section might look like this:

```
                        Personal information ❷

Name: JOE Q. CONSUMER                 SSN: XXX-XX-6789 ❷
Other names: CONSUMER, JOSEPH Q.
Report number: XXXXXXX ❷              Date of birth: 04/1965
Report date: April 4, 2017           Telephone number(s): 917-555-1212


CURRENT ADDRESS: ❷                    PREVIOUS ADDRESSES:
123 MAIN ST., NEW YORK, NY 12345      17 BROOKLYN AVE., LONG ISLAND, NY 56789

EMPLOYMENT DATA REPORTED ❷            Position: PROGRAMMER
Employer name: CREDITCARDS.COM        Hired: 05/2011
Location: New York, NY               Position:
Date reported: 06/2012               Hired: 03/2007
Employer name: UNIVERSITY OF TEXAS
Location: TX
Date reported: 08/2008
```

Much of the information displayed in this section comes from the data you provide when making a loan and other credit applications. For this reason, it is of the utmost importance that you are forthcoming, accurate, and consistent in the information that you provide. Falsifying data provided during loan application is criminal and may be grounds for prosecution.

Information category 2: Monthly reported accounts

The next category of information will consist of data provided by creditors who file monthly status reports. This will usually include anyone who receives a monthly payment from you that is meant to clear all or part of your credit, such as:

- Commercial lenders such as banks, credit unions, credit card companies, savings and loans institutions, student loan providers, etc.

- Credit issuers that can be classified as non-bank. Examples include: Carte Blanche, Diner's Club, American Express

- Department stores

- Utility companies

Information in this section will usually contain the following:

- Name of lender

- Payment history

- Date of account opening

- Account numbers

- Type of debt (revolving, installment debt, open debt)

- The balance on the account

- Your limits

- The responsibility you have on the account is a joint account, an individual account. Are you an authorized user?

Now, **the** information in this section tends to be detailed, especially in instances where your account is handed over to another party, such as another creditor or debt collector. As such, you may see two or more institutions listed under the same credit account. Such separate reports are called trade-lines.

A more realistic version of this section may look like the one below:

Accounts in good standing, satisfactory accounts ❷

GMAC FINANCING #640006137129

78901 JENKINS CIR
FLOOR 15
MIAMI, FL 33025
Phone number not available

Balance: $1,145
Date updated: 08/2017
High balance: $10,000
Collateral: 2009 Dodge
RamCredit limit: $10,000
Past due: $0
Terms: $295 for 36 months

Pay status: Pays as agreed ❷
Account type: Installment account
Responsibility: Individual account
Date opened: 11/2013
Date closed: 11/2016
Date paid: 11/2016

Loan type: Automobile
Remarks: Paid by insurance
Estimated date that this item will be removed: 12/2023

Information category 3: Accounts reported with negative information

Now, the previous section will contain information on accounts that you are **on** good terms with.

This is not usually the case with most people. There are some accounts with which you may have defaulted or fallen behind in payments. Information on such accounts is listed in this section.

Information in this category will typically consist of:

- The name of the lender or creditor (the original one or the one who took over your account)

- Type of credit

- Your account number

- Your responsibility

- Your status with regards to your delinquency

Note: Failed or late child support payments can also appear in this section.

Once again, you should expect a section filled with information that resembles the picture below.

Information Category 4: Public Information

This section will include data about your special interest to creditors, and that is public knowledge. It is public knowledge because it has been filed by the local, state, or federal government. Relevant items may include the following:

- A bankruptcy
- A foreclosure
- Lawsuits
- Divorces
- Evictions
- Court judgments
- Tax liens

Here is a screenshot of what you might find in this section.

Public records ⊘

ROCKWELL MUNICIPAL Docket #: 9B004875

| 5468 MLK AVE., SUITE 300, ROCKWELL, TX 97845 | **Type:** Civil judgment **Court type:** Municipal **Date paid:** 07/2012 **Assets:** $1,089 | **Date filed:** 12/2011 **Responsibility:** Participant on account **Plaintiff:** BANK OF TEXAS **Plaintiff attorney:** RICHARD PERRY **Amount:** $1,089 |

Estimated date that this item will be removed 07/2019 ⊘

Information category 5: Inquiries

Lastly, you have a category of inquiries.

Inquiries refer to requests by parties to access your credit history. Any number of parties may request your credit report. The most common ones include:

- Commercial lenders
- Mortgage lenders
- Utility companies

- Landlords

- Student loan lenders

- Insurers

- Employers

- Government agencies

- Collection agencies

- Parties that have a court order

Now, regarding inquiries. It is important to note that there are two types of inquiries:

- Hard inquiries are submitted by entities such as your insurance company, your creditors. Hard inquiries can and do affect your credit score.

- Soft inquiries, on the other hand, do not affect your credit score. They may be submitted by creditors trying to check your status, either for promotions, yourself, or your employers.

Here's what you may expect to see in a real section detailing inquiries.

Credit history requests @

CALTECH EMPLOYEE FCU

555 W. ADAMS
SUITE 202
LA CANADA, CA 91012
(818) 555-1212

Requested on: 11/01/2017
Inquiry type: Individual @

Permissible purpose: Credit
transaction @

SUNSHINE APARTMENTS via RENTPORT

678 MARINE STREET
SUITE 999
LOS ANGELES, CA 90210
(818) 555-1212

Requested on: 05/01/2016
Inquiry type: Individual
Loan type: Real estate

Permissible purpose: Tenant
screening @

CHASE CARD MEMBER SVCS

666 W. SMITH
PHOENIX, AZ 87853
Phone number not available

Requested on: 11/01/2016
Inquiry type: Individual

Your Credit Scores And What They Imply

The last way to examine your financial situation is to look at your credit score.

A credit score is a 3-digit number that is derived from your credit report. It is supposed to tell a creditor, at a glance, just how likely you are to pay back whatever amount they lend you.

In other words, a credit score is a shortcut - a summary - of your credit report. And knowing what your score means is just as important as looking at your credit report.

Generally, the higher your credit score is, the better. A high credit score is an indication that you are likely to pay your debt in good time. This means you get lent money at the best terms, at the lowest interest rates, with low fees.

Conversely, if your credit score is low, it is an indication that you have a bad credit history. You likely have gotten into trouble with credit before and are likely to do so again. Thus, you are perceived as a high-risk borrower.

Depending on the policy or business model a lender is working with, you may be denied credit or get lent money at very stringent terms.

Now, it is worth noting that credit scores are arrived at by applying a series of proprietary mathematical formulas and comparing you to other people with good or bad credit histories.

Proprietary means secret - the details about the formulas' workings are not revealed to the public, except for the companies that apply them.

This doesn't mean that you are at a loss. The fact of the matter is that the factors taken into account when applying these formulas and the weight they carry is not that much of a secret. Improving on those factors is your ticket to improving your credit score.

And with that, seven major players are involved in the business of calculating credit reporting and scoring.

THE BIG PLAYERS IN CREDIT REPORTING AND SCORING

To make it easy for you to follow and differentiate seven major players, I will categorize them into three categories.

The major credit reporting agencies that are regulated by Fair Credit Reporting Act

1. Experian

2. Transunion

3. Equifax

Specialty Credit Reporting Agencies

1. LexisNexis

2. Chex Systems

Credit Scoring Companies

1. FICO

2. VantageScore

Let's discuss each of these in detail.

The Major Credit Reporting Agencies Regulated By The Fair Credit Reporting Act

1: Experian

The first major credit reporting agency is called Experian.

This company first came to life in 1996 when it went public on the London Stock Exchange. It currently trades under the symbol EXPN.

Before then, it was owned by several companies such as TRW Inc., Bain Capital, Thomas H. Lee Partners, and later, The Great Universal Stores Limited (GUS).

GUS, a retail conglomerate that maintained tens of millions of customers, made Experian what it is today. A database was designed around that data, and that formed the core asset of the company.

Today, the company has its headquarters in Dublin, in Ireland. It keeps credit information records belonging to over 1 billion people from 37 countries. Included in that massive database are records of over 235 million active credit consumers in the United States and over 25 million businesses here in America.

2: Equifax

The next authoritative force in the credit reporting business is Equifax, which trades in the New York Stock Exchange under EFX.

The company has a rich history, having been founded in 1899 by Cator Woolford and Guy Woolford. Back then, it was known as Retail Credit Company.

The name was later changed to Equifax in 1975, reportedly to improve its image, which had been tainted by a series of public allegations about privacy violations. Those allegations led Congress to pass the Fair Credit Reporting Act.

Today, it is a multinational that operates in 24 countries located in Europe, the Americas, and the Asia Pacific.

It keeps credit records belonging to over 800 million people and 88 million businesses worldwide, and its headquarters are found in Atlanta, Georgia.

3: TransUnion

The final company on the list of the major credit reporting agencies is Transunion, which also happens to be the smallest of the three.

The company had its origins in 1968 when it operated as the Union Tank Car Company's holding company – a railroad leasing operation.

Later, the company bought the Credit Bureau of Cook County, which had a list of 3.6 million credit accounts under its possession. This was the beginning of the firm operating as a reporting agency.

Transunion would later be sold off to the Marmon Group, which would then sell it to Madison Dearborn Partners. Later in 2010, Goldman Sachs, along with

Advent International, would buy it before taking it public in 2015.

It currently trades in the New York Stock Exchange under the symbol TRU.

Transunion is reported to maintain over 1 billion individual credit consumers worldwide in over 30 countries. An estimated 200 million of them are American Consumers. Also included in that list are over 65,000 businesses.

The headquarters are located in Chicago, Illinois.

Specialty Credit Reporting Agencies

Besides the three major credit reporting organizations controlled by the Fair Credit Reporting Act that we have discussed, we also have known as specialty credit reporting agencies.

These are organizations that perform the same role of collecting and reporting information. The difference is that they specialize in very specific niches such as banking, insurance, medical, auto, etc.

For this book's purposes, we will look at two major firms that play a pivotal role in specialty credit reporting – LexisNexis and Chex Systems.

1: LexisNexis

LexisNexis is a credit reporting agency that has its headquarters based in Ontario, Toronto, Canada.

John Horty founded the company in early 1956. His original intention was to build a database that would keep track of differing hospital administration laws across states in the U.S.

The project would later attract other parties' interests, keep contributing to it, and make it the organization it is today.

At the time of this writing, LexisNexis holds the largest database in existence that keeps track of legal matters and public records.

This means that this company is in a unique position to report information on the following:

- Your real estate transactions - House ownership and how much was paid

- Your tax liens

- Judgments

- Bankruptcies

- The professional licenses you have

- Insurance claims

- Historical addresses

It is important to note that LexisNexis is still governed by the Fair Credit Reporting Act that affords you the right to ask for a free report once, every 12 months. You also have the right to dispute any wrong information you find in that document.

If you are interested in getting a hold of your LexisNexis report, there are three ways you can do that:

- You can place your request online through the company's consumer portal at https://consumer.risk.lexisnexis.com/request. You can find instructions on how to place such a request here[1].

1　　　https://consumer.risk.lexisnexis.com/img/Electronic_Request_Form_Instructions.pdf

- You can fill out a form that you **download here**[2] and mail it to the company at this address:

LexisNexis Risk Solutions Consumer Center

P.O. BOX 105108

Atlanta, GA 30348-5108

If they honor your request, your report will arrive via mail.

- And lastly, you can place a phone call to +1 866 897 8126

2: Chex Systems

The next type of specialty credit reporting agency worth looking at is ChexSystems.

The company that owns it is called eFunds, which is a subsidiary of Fidelity National Information Services.

ChexSystems specializes in providing reports on banking. Specifically, ChexSystems collects data on your checking and savings accounts, prepares reports on your activities, and sells the information to banking institutions.

The idea is to give a more accurate picture of your risk profile.

Suppose there are serious issues in how you've managed your banking accounts, such as failing to pay account fees, too many overdrafts, unsettled accounts, fraud, and other issues that lead to account closure. In that case, that information is usually picked up by ChexSystems.

---

2   https://consumer.risk.lexisnexis.com/img/LexisNexis_ Report_Request_Form.pdf

ChexSystems gets its divine intel by collaborating with banks so that they install software to monitor your banking behavior in real-time. It is estimated that 80 percent of all commercial banks and credit unions in America participate in this kind of symbiotic relationship.

You know that you're in trouble when an application to open a new account is declined. In that case, if you inquire about being given reasons, you may find out that you have a negative entry in your credit report that has made you a risky proposition in the eyes of the bank or credit union.

If this happens, you can **request a ChexSystems report**[3], which should be afforded to you for free, once every 12 months. You can then look through the data displayed and identify areas where the real issues arise, and seek ways to address them so that you can get back to having a good relationship with the financial world.

You also get to know about your score because ChexSystems, like other reporting agencies, also generates a score that ranges between 100 and 899. And generally, the higher your score is, the lower the risk you present to banking and credit institutions.

However, it is important to realize that unless you get into trouble with opening new bank accounts, items on your ChexSystems report and your score don't matter in the grand scheme of things. They also have no direct impact on your overall credit score.

---

3   https://www.chexsystems.com/web/chexsystems/consumerdebit/otherpage/FACTAFreeReport/

Now that you have a good understanding of the different credit reporting agencies let's now look at the companies that provide credit scoring solutions.

The Major Credit Scoring Companies

Look at a typical credit report for any given period. You will realize that credit reports from different credit reporting agencies will often be different for the same period. This is because they use different credit scoring formulas, depending on the credit scoring company they use.

Two major companies are in the business of credit scoring using their proprietary formulas.

1: FICO

FICO stands for Fair Isaac Corporation.

It is a company that was founded by Bill Fair and Earl Isaac back in 1956. Back then, it was known as Fair Isaac and Company.

The two founders were both workers at the Stanford Research Institute based in Menlo Park, California. Bill Fair was an engineer, and Earl Isaac, a mathematician.

The two worked to develop a computerized model that could analyze data stored in credit reports. The intention was to produce scores that could predict a borrower's risk of default.

The effort proved fruitful since the credit scoring system was quickly adopted after single pitching to 50 American lenders.

The company went public in 1986 and has been listed on the New York Stock Exchange since then. The name would later be changed to Fair Isaac Corporation in 2003.

Today, the company has its headquarters in San Jose, California.

And in the credit scoring space, this company is king since it is estimated that 90% of lenders in America today rely on FICO scores to base their decisions. FICO has developed the FICO scoring model, which is relied on by the majority of the lenders.

Therefore, it is likely that the lender you seek to get a mortgage or auto loan from will rely on this model to make decisions.

How to access your FICO score

One thing to note is that, unlike credit reports, you usually don't gain access to your scores without paying. There are, however, apps out there - which we will look into in a moment - which will let you check your credit score for free.

That said, the preferred way to access your FICO score is through a website called **myfico.com**. The website features a subscription service that allows you – in addition to receiving monthly credit score reports - to gain access to other complementary services such as:

- Identity theft insurance

- Scores for other industries such as auto, mortgages, etc.

- Credit reporting.

It is essential to realize that FICO scores are made available from all three major credit bureaus because data kept by all these three significant firms about your credit history is not the same.

Thus, Equifax's score will be close to but will not resemble that from TransUnion.

And with that, it's time we talked of your score and what it likely implies about your credit situation.

You need to keep in mind that FICO scores range from a low of 300 to 850.

As a rule, the higher your score, the healthier your credit profile is.

But, as a matter of convenience, this is how creditors usually interpret your FICO scores:

1. *300 – 579 (Very Poor)*

If your score belongs in this category, you are doing very poorly for your situation. The worst possible category you can ever belong to. Most creditors won't take even a second look at you with this kind of score.

Those who do will be demanding high fees as well as mandatory deposits. And that is without saying anything about interest charges, which will usually be abnormally high as well.

2. *580 – 669 (Fair)*

Belonging in this category is undoubtedly a lot better than being at the bottom of the pile.

Usually, Lenders have a fancy term for borrowers in this category. That term is a subprime borrower.

A subprime borrower is a high-risk borrower who usually gets lent money at less than stellar credit terms.

The good news is that some borrowers will consider you. The bad news is, not many of them will be willing to take on such a risk. Subprime lending is a niche market. And the sad thing is that the biggest and most reputable lenders are not big players in this kind of game. So, you are left with the least reputable lenders who are notorious for offering the most expensive loans.

3. *670 – 739 (Good)*

If you are in this category, you are doing better than most credit-wise. Experian estimates that only 2 out of every ten people have a credit score that falls within this range.

And many lenders will consider you, mainly because they figure that a modest 8% of people who fall within this category are likely to default or become notoriously delinquent.

4. *740 – 799 (Very Good)*

If you belong here, your credit is in good shape. Also, many lenders are itching to do business with you. Because of your low-risk proposition, lenders are usually willing to lend to you at better than average rates.

5. *800 – 850 (Exceptional)*

Belonging in this category is the equivalent of making a perfect score on an SAT. Usually, you gain admission into the best schools and get accepted to take the most prestigious course programs.

It is the same with lenders - people in this category top every lender's list. They are all too happy to do business with you. And at the best terms possible. When you are in this category, life is good.

With all that we've learned in mind, let me briefly discuss a New FICO scoring model, widely known as FICO Resilience Index.

The New FICO Resilience Index

Let's spend some time talking about a new credit scoring model that has surfaced to help lenders make wiser credit decisions during periods of economic crisis.

Lenders have long known that the economy is expected to go through periods of boom and bust.

They also know that borrowers present different risk profiles during each cycle.

To minimize risk default and consequently lose money, creditors understand that they need to be conservative during recessions and optimistic during good times.

To this end, they have sought to establish models that will help them make more informed lending decisions. And in the wake of the Covid-19 pandemic, one model that has been welcomed with open arms is the New Fico Resilience Index.

The New FICO Resilience index is a scoring model that serves to measure an individual's ability to weather economic storms and still honor their financial obligations.

It works by taking into account the prototypical factors used in any other scoring model, such as:

- The balance on accounts

- Your payment history

- Type of credit

- Credit utilization ratio

- The age of credit

- New inquiries

The whole point of having this index is to prevent a scenario where people with healthy credit and good financial habits end up being unfairly assessed during a period of economic strain.

That is, lenders still want worthy borrowers to have a chance at accessing credit easily and at reasonable terms, even though their financial outlook may have taken a bruising.

The standard scoring models will be taken into account, but lenders also realize the limitations of these models. So, to be cautious and still be fair simultaneously, this model will come in handy.

You will need to keep in mind two peculiar things with this new scoring model, though. First, unlike the standard one, this one generates a two-digit score ranging from 1 to 99.

Second, the higher the score, the higher the risk presented by the individual. This contrasts with other traditional models' implications, which generally associate a lower risk profile with higher ratings.

With that in mind, a score that ranges between 1 and 44 implies an individual with high resilience to economic downturns, which makes them an acceptable risk to the financial institutions.

On the other hand, a score that begins at 70 and peaks at 100 implies an individual with low tolerance to economic risk and is likely to default on loans and other forms of credit offered to them.

Interesting stuff, eh?

So how do you get access to your New FICO Resilience Index Report and score?

Well, the sad news is that this new scoring model is in its initial stages of implementation, and mechanisms haven't been put in place yet to allow normal credit consumers to gain access to their data on demand.

But, that will change as time goes by.

In the meantime, just acknowledge the existence of this new scoring model.

Also, keep in mind that this in no way suggests that you should deviate from classical financial habits and borrowing practices that have been known to keep you in good graces with lenders.

There are no new secrets to game the system. The rules of the game remain the same.

The other big player in credit scoring is VantageScore Solutions. Let's learn that next.

2: VantageScore Solutions

Throughout the years, FICO monopolized the credit scoring business.

Then, in 2006, in a joint effort involving the three major credit bureaus (Equifax, Experian, and Transunion), a scoring model known as VantageScore was developed.

The intention was to provide a scoring model that competed in the marketplace and provided greater reliability and accuracy.

Ever since its inception, four versions of this model have been developed and marketed.

They are:

- VantageScore 1.0

- VantageScore 2.0

- VantageScore 3.0

- VantageScore 4.0

VantageScore Solutions LLC is the company that holds the intellectual property rights to the scoring model. All three major credit reporting giants own the company.

Let's learn more about the VantageScore credit scoring model.

You will recall mentioning that the three major credit bureaus created this model to compete directly with FICO in the credit score market.

They haven't done a very good job of that since 90% of lenders still rely on the FICO score. Nevertheless,

VantageScore's popularity has increased amongst certain groups such as credit card companies, auto dealers, and landlords.

If you want access to this score, you will have to order one through each of the major credit bureau's official website.

A key difference between VantageScore and FICO is that it takes up to six months of credit history for the model to come up with a score with the latter. Otherwise, the data is deemed insufficient.

VantageScore gets around that problem by allowing calculations to take place within a month or two.

Thus, if you don't have much of credit history, but wish to be scored, then VantageScore offers much hope for you.

That said, let's examine what different scoring ranges will mean to lenders. Keep in mind that, like FICO, this model produces scores ranging from 300 t0 850.

In the past, the highest range in this model was 990. However, confusion among lenders and borrowers brought about the need for changes to the model. It compares directly with that of FICO, which most people are familiar with.

That is not meant to indicate that the algorithm involved in calculating VantageScore is the same as that of FICO. There are some slight variations in the weight given to factors, which set the two apart.

With that in mind, implications of the different scores produced by this model include the following:

1. *300 – 499 (Very Poor)*

Once again, this is as low as you can go. Almost no reputable lender will have any incentive to do business with you.

2. *500 – 600 (Poor)*

Not too bad, but also not good enough. You might get a few lenders to look in your direction, but they won't be enthusiastic. For those who will have any interest, the lending conditions will be unfavorable. Large down-payments, as well as exorbitant interest rates, should be expected.

3. *601 – 660 (Fair)*

Much better. Lenders will be open to deal with you, but understandably at higher interest rates.

4. *661 - 780 (Good)*

Now you are in good territory. The vast majority of lenders are happy to lend to you and at favorable rates.

5. *781 – 850 (Excellent)*

If your score belongs here, you are in the big leagues. You can think of yourself as one of the "chosen ones." You get priority consideration. And when times are good, the best offers in the credit industry will come your way.

FREE CREDIT-MONITORING APPS

At this point, you understand that without a doubt, you need to monitor your credit regularly, given the much that is riding on them.

We've talked about the various paid options you can use to access your credit score as well as credit reports. But what if you could exercise some free options and save some money?

The good news is that such options do exist. And here they are:

1. *Credit Karma*

This is arguably one of the best free options out there.

The app has versions for both Android and IOS platforms. You can also access the service through your PC or laptop browser.

Among the app features, access to credit reports and scores from both Equifax and TransUnion (of the VantageScore variety) every week ranks high in that list.

Others include tools for saving or tax preparation.

The business model that underlies this app involves targeted advertisements as well as recommendations to app users. The operators get a share of the proceeds if you happen to purchase any of the products or services it recommends.

2. *Mint*

Mint, from software giant Intuit, is yet another force to reckon with.

It is an app that allows you to do your budgeting, track your expenses, plan your finances, and monitor your credit, all in one place.

It is important to note that this app will only provide you with free credit data that updates only once a month. Once again, it is worth noting that scores provided by this app come from the VantageScore model.

3. *Credit Sesame*

Then, there is Credit Sesame, which only focuses on managing debt. Unlike other service providers who focus on more holistic service-offerings, Credit Sesame only specializes in financial liabilities.

As you might expect, the service also provides credit scores and reports. These scores are the VantageScore variety and come from TransUnion.

The operators can offer free service because they make money from product and service endorsements from players in the financial world. These endorsements are uniquely tailored to suit each individual's situation that holds an account with the app.

4. *CreditWise*

Lastly, but not least, you have the option of using CreditWise from credit giant Capital One.

The app allows you to check your credit scores and TransUnion reports, which are updated every week.

Perhaps at this point, you can begin to understand why many people see different scores on these apps from the ones they see when making actual loan or credit card applications with a lender.

As I've pointed out, most (roughly 90%) lenders rely on FICO scores.

Conversely, practically every free credit monitoring app out there offers scores from VantageScore or TransUnion. The differences in the two models account for much of the disparity in the aforementioned credit scores.

PART 2:

FIXING YOUR CREDIT

The previous part has covered the fundamentals of credit exhaustively. You now know where you stand credit-wise.

In this part, we will look at how you can fix your situation for the better. If your credit is in bad shape, we will look at ways to build it and make it better.

If you have no credit history, we will talk about how you can build credit in the quickest way possible. We will also look at how you can safely leverage the credit system without posing serious risks to your credit profile.

So let's get to it.

Building A Better Credit Profile

Building a better credit profile is usually a matter of two things – fixing your credit report errors and taking actions to improve your credit score.

We will look at each one of these steps in turn. Let's begin with the first one.

i. Fixing errors in your report

This may come as news to you, but often credit reports contain errors that are detrimental to your credit score. This is the case, time and again.

An estimated 30% of accounts maintained by credit bureaus have serious errors that will warrant denial of credit in the eyes of lenders who proceed under the assumption that they are factual.

Therefore, it pays to investigate your credit report thoroughly to determine whether there are problems in it that need fixing.

In other cases, it has to do with your profile being incomplete. That is, there might be missing information in certain sections of your report.

The Fair Credit Reporting Act (FCRA) gives you legal rights to dispute or raise concerns about your credit report items that need altering.

That said, there are popular categories of errors that you should be on the lookout for a while examining your credit report. They include:

1. ***Personal Data Section***

Common errors in this section usually take on the following forms:

- The name, address, or phone number fields are either incomplete or contain incorrect data. Such as someone else's.

- No presence of your previous address in case you moved recently.

- Your data about employment is either inaccurate or non-existent.

- The social security number or birth date do not belong to you.

- The marital status is not reflective of your current situation.

2. ***Public Information Section***

Errors in this part will usually include:

- Lawsuits you never partook in.

- Bankruptcies that were filed by persons other than yourself - for instance, your spouse.

- Tax liens that were paid over seven years ago.

- Bankruptcies were filed over ten years ago.

- Bankruptcies that have not been identified by a specific chapter.

- Lawsuits or judgments over seven years old.

- Arrest records that go far back to over seven years

- Other liens are itemized as unpaid when you paid them off.

3. *Reported accounts section*

Mistakes usually uncovered in this part include:

- Negative information (such as failed child support payments or delinquent accounts) is more than seven years old.

- A tradeline that doesn't indicate turning over your account to a collection agency, giving the impression of another overdue account.

- The date of delinquency on certain accounts is inaccurate.

- A delinquent account that doesn't list the date.

- Accounts that are listed as "open" when, in fact, you had them closed. Giving the impression that you have many open lines of credit.

- Accounts that list you as a cosigner when you weren't.

- Accounts that are listed as closed by the lender, when you had them closed yourself.

- A vehicle repossession that was, in fact, a voluntary surrender on your part.

- A charge on a card that you disputed and that doesn't indicate that fact.

- Debts associated with bankruptcies that don't have a zero balance.

- Failure to show debts that were discharged through bankruptcy.

- Debts listed as yours, which belonged to your spouse before your marriage.

- Debts accounts that were the result of identity theft.

- Accounts that do not indicate that you are only an authorized user.

- Downright misleading information on credit history. For instance, late payment on accounts that were paid on time.

- Joint accounts that you never cosigned on.

- Credit history entries belong to someone else, who may have a similar name, but who isn't you.

4. *Inquiries section*

Here, issues usually involve listings of automobile sellers or businesses that chose to run a credit check without your written consent.

As you can see, there is a whole barrel-full of items with issues to cross-examine in your credit report. Be sure to be thorough in your search of items that could be disputed.

Now, on disputing incorrect information, your job is to write to the credit bureau, requesting the takedown of the false information.

At that point, one of two things will likely happen:

- The credit agency promptly deletes the incorrect information from your report.

- The credit agency agrees to conduct a reinvestigation of the matters brought forth by you.

If the agency decides to take the first course of action, it should do so in 3 days. Also, it should notify you by way of telephone, send a confirmation letter, along with a copy of the updated credit report.

If, on the other hand, the agency finds it appropriate to conduct a reinvestigation before it corrects the disputed information, then it should do so within a matter of 30 days. It's also worth pointing out that you should receive a report of what was uncovered five days into the investigation.

The only exception to this rule is if you disputed the information after receiving your annual free report. In that case, 45 days becomes the maximum allowed timespan.

ii. Improving Your Credit Score

Improving your credit score is a matter of capitalizing on the scoring companies' factors when calculating your score.

This means that you must understand what those factors are to succeed in becoming responsible with your credit or even getting yourself out of trouble.

You will recall that I mentioned before that the factors used to calculate credit scores by both FICO and VantageScore models are essentially the same. Only the weightings given to each factor are different. It is also important to note that these differences are not far apart.

Keeping these important facts in mind is useful because the rules of improving your credit scores are practically the same no matter what credit scoring model you are using to evaluate yourself.

So, let's quickly go over the factors that generally go into determining your credit score before discussing the rules and strategies for improving your credit score. Here they are:

- Your credit payment history

- Your debt utilization ratio

- The type as well as several inquiries on your report

- The number of credit accounts opened in the recent past

- The type of public records out there on you such as bankruptcy

- The total amount of debt you have

- The type of credit accounts you hold

- The age of your credit accounts

How well you align your character and behavior with the above factors ultimately determines how well you fair on your credit score.

With that in mind, here are the rules you should follow if you want to have stellar credit:

1. ***Make sure your bills and debts are paid on time***

Here's something you need to know: your debt payment history carries the greatest amount of weight for both scoring models.

No other factor overrides this simple fact. The way the creditors see it, someone who can pay his or her bills on time, settle credit card balances, or any other type of loan is someone who has got their act together.

Such a person likely makes a good income, hasn't overstretched themselves, and is deserving of a good score.

This should bring home a key lesson; if you get nothing else out of this book other than the idea that you should pay your bills and debt balances on time, it will have been a worthwhile endeavor.

Now, this may be a challenge given the committed nature of today's life. You may be too busy handling other obligations to the point of forgetting simple but important elements like dates that you should pay your bill.

The good news is that there are tools out there that can help you with this. One option you have is setting up automatic payments. This excellent article from **Money Under 30** will give you excellent tips and instructions on how you can set automatic payments up.

Another option you have is setting up calendar notifications. Most smartphones phones allow you to do this. You can either use the native apps that come with the phone or download a third-party app such as Google Calendar.

2. *Maintain low balances on credit cards and other revolving credit*

Interestingly enough, lenders do not like seeing you max out on all options they give you. Yes, they do want to lend you their money. But, if you want to appear valuable in front of their eyes, you can't take all of it. You have to take just a small portion of it.

Your lenders will be keen on your credit utilization ratio to keep tabs on your ability to do this. This figure measures the amount of debt load you are carrying as a percentage of your overall credit limit.

The higher your credit utilization ratio, the more negative your picture looks in the eyes of lenders. This is especially the case if you are a heavy consumer of revolving debt – you know - like credit cards.

To illustrate what I mean here, let us look at the formula for calculating your credit utilization ratio:

$$Credit\ utilization\ ratio = \frac{Total\ balance\ on\ cards}{Total\ limits\ on\ cards} \times 100\%$$

So let's say the total balance on all your cards this month amounts to $2,500. And your math also happens to reveal to you that your limits on all cards at your disposal stands at $10,000.

Based on the formula above, your credit utilization ratio is 25%.

Now, typically most lenders prefer that your credit utilization ratio stays below 30%. The lower the number, the better.

The basic logic behind all this is that someone who has a low credit utilization ratio isn't credit-dependent and has a healthy financial outlook.

So, do your math and establish your credit utilization ratio. If it is high, find ways to start paying off those balances as soon as possible until your ratio drops to a healthy level. Your credit score will benefit a great deal from such an effort.

3. *Keep from opening new credit accounts unnecessarily*

Given the knowledge you currently have about credit utilization ratio, you might seek to lower it by applying for new credit cards to raise your total credit limit.

What a great idea!

Unfortunately, things are never that simple. Applying for new credit is a double-edged sword. While you might succeed in raising your overall credit limit, your credit score will suffer from the impact of hard inquiries.

Remember, any time you apply for credit, your lender (or prospective lender) conducts a hard inquiry for them to get a picture of your overall credit situation.

Hard inquiries, as a rule, lower your credit scores, and for a good reason. The more you apply for new credit, the more likely you don't have your financial situation under control. Lenders use this as a signal that implies that you are becoming more credit risk.

The important point to note here is that the strategy of applying for new credit in a bid to raise your score is one that will cost you a lot more than it is worth. So, only apply for new credit when you need it.

4. *Keep unused credit cards open*

Now, here's another neat trick you can add to your list:

If you took several credit lines in the past but currently have paid them off and have little or no use for them, avoid closing those accounts.

Yes, this might sound counterintuitive, but it works. I'll explain.

It goes back to the credit utilization ratio issue. By default, having many open lines of credit means that your credit limit is bigger. And if you don't make any use of those accounts, your credit utilization ratio gets smaller.

All these two work in your favor in getting a more desirable credit score.

You might be thinking, "Doesn't having numerous open lines of credit increase the temptation to use them?"

Sure it does.

But there is a way around that issue and one that I recommend highly. It is this - Simply cut up credit cards representing accounts that you do not use.

Yes, destroy them. That way, you cannot use them. Meanwhile, your accounts remain open. Your lenders will keep them open until you request to have them closed – an action you must never consider under any circumstance as long as it doesn't cost you much (or anything) to keep them open.

There's also another side benefit to keeping unused accounts open. They age. Recall that the length of credit history is also factored into the equation. So, the older your accounts, the better.

Someone who has a long credit history will certainly have a better score than someone who has only started borrowing money recently.

This is a great way to kill two birds with one stone.

5. *Dispute erroneous entries in your reports*

This has been the subject of the previous section.

I can't stress its importance enough. Creditors, sometimes out of sheer negligence or outright misconduct, submit entries to inaccurate credit companies.

You cannot - and should - not let the mistakes and misdeeds of creditors and other stakeholders in the credit party determine your fate. You have to carefully cross-examine reports to ascertain whether they are representative of you and your past.

6. *Boost your score by submitting utility and cell phone bill payments*

I reserved this option for the last because it is a unique offering.

If you can prove on-time payments of utility and electric bills, Experian can boost your credit score for free.

You just have to follow this link[4] and sign up for the service. According to Experian, the service will link to your bank accounts to obtain verifiable evidence of your cell phone and utility bills.

Once that is done, you will be prompted to confirm that you indeed wish to have the discovered data added to your file. If the data reveals that you are compliant, both your VantageScore and FICO credit score variants will benefit appreciably.

Now you are equipped with knowledge about the ways and means you can improve your credit score. Perhaps you are a new credit consumer and are interested in:

Establishing Credit For The First Time

Let's say you have what is often referred to as a *"thin credit file"* in the industry.

In other words, you either have very little credit history to back you or simply have none at all.

What do you do?

Keep in mind that most lenders will not give their money to someone who has no history with credit. Such a person is way too unpredictable for them to take any chances with.

If you are in this position, I have both good news and bad news. I'll start with the good news.

First, realize that there is much hope for you. It's a lot easier for someone who has no credit to build a

---

4   https://www.experian.com/blogs/ask-experian/credit-education/improving-credit/improve-credit-score/

healthy credit profile compared to someone who needs to get rid of blemishes like bankruptcy in their credit.

You will be delighted to find out that there are steps that you can take today. And if you behave yourself accordingly, you'll have a healthy credit to leverage in a year or two.

Now, for the bad news. The overwhelming truth is that there is no shortcut to building credit.

There is no magical hack. It can't be done overnight. You will need the patience to put in the effort and wait.

But as they say, "All good things come to those who wait." If you take the correct steps and are patient, eventually, you will reap the rewards of a good to excellent credit.

That said, what are some of the actions you can take to build credit from scratch?

i. Get a secured credit card

One of the best ways to get started with building credit is by using a secured credit card.

As the name sounds, this is a special type of credit card in which the debt offered is protected against default by some type of security. That security, in this case, is a deposit.

Here's the point you will need to understand: when you apply for a secured credit card and are prompted to provide a deposit, the amount you offer up will not only act as collateral in the event of default, it also acts as your credit limit.

Put another way, if you apply for a secured card and are asked to provide a $1,000 security deposit, it merely implies that you are extended credit up to that amount.

Now, when you terminate that account or switch up to a secured credit card, you can get your deposit refunded.

So you might want to go out there and try to get a secured credit card.

ii. Ask to be made an authorized user

Another great option that helps you build your credit involves leveraging someone else's credit card account.

This can be an excellent strategy, especially if the other person in question has good credit and is responsible for your finances.

So, if you have a family member or a close friend who fits the profile, this is a viable option for you.

The way to make this happen is to head up to the lender who has issued your chosen candidate with credit and ask them to sign you up as an authorized user of their card.

As you do this, be sure to confirm that the card's issuer will submit reports of your role as an authorized user to credit rating agencies.

One way to confirm that this is the case is to check whether you are asked to provide your Social Security Number during the sign-up process. If you are not prompted to give up this information, then your arrangement will not benefit your credit in any way, and your efforts are likely a waste of time.

The good thing about this strategy is that you won't even have to use the card. As long as the other person uses and pays bills on the card regularly without making mistakes, your credit will benefit from it.

On the downside, if the other person overextends their use of credit, fails to pay bills on time, or commits any number of credit crimes that usually land people into trouble, your credit will suffer for it.

So be sure to be picky when selecting an ideal person to work with.

iii. Get a cosigner to help you take out a loan.

There is yet another way to get around the issue of lenders not wanting to extend credit without a score – get someone to cosign on a loan.

A cosigner is someone who puts a signature on your loan application, effectively guaranteeing payment of debt should you fail or become unable to pay the money back.

In other words, someone is legally vouching for you. They are backing their confidence in you by placing their credit on the line.

Here's what I mean: in the event of you defaulting on the loan, not only is the co-signer obligated to pay, their credit takes a hit as well.

This option is not that as exciting as it sounds because you have to get a loan now; if you could use a loan to, say, start a business or finance the purchase of a car, fine.

However, if you have no real need for credit, this could be a tempting option to make money available for spending when you haven't earned it yet.

As you can reasonably surmise, this is a tightrope to walk on. It has the potential to put you into debt problems and ruin your relationship with the cosigner you've chosen.

So, careful deliberation is a vital requirement when considering this choice.

iv. Student loan

Yet another unexpected way to start building credit is through getting a student loan.

As you probably already know, student loans are available to persons with little or even no credit.

If you are just starting in life, this is a great way to start building credit. On the one hand, the education you acquire will be of immense value throughout your life. This is a good thing.

On the other hand, once you are done with your education, you start proving your value to creditors.

I can't think of many situations where you end up with positive outcomes like that.

But there is one caveat. If you borrow excessively without having much of a repayment plan, student loans can be quite a burden. As we speak, student loans are a big problem for many young people who find that they are likely to service a huge debt for much of their adult life.

Student debt is beneficial if you can properly plan for a well-paying career that you are committed to. Also, your odds of succeeding need to be good enough so that you will likely offset the downside risk associated with the loan you are taking.

v. Get a store credit card

Many retail stores such as Kohl's, Neiman Marcus, Lord and Taylor, Saks Fifth Avenue, and others issue cards to shoppers to buy items on credit.

Usually, getting these cards is not very difficult because you don't need an excellent score to qualify.

It's another option to consider, especially when you have few options for getting credit.

One thing to keep in mind is that you must never use this card to buy things you cannot afford. Doing so will almost certainly destroy your score.

What you want to do with this card is deliberately shop for something with it when you are certain that you have the cash to pay it back. I recommend that you have the cash in hand to pay for an artifact before you use it.

For you, this is just a way for you to build credit. Not to get yourself into credit problems when you don't have to.

I trust that you will find these five options very instrumental in your journey towards building credit from scratch.

Remember, at the very least, it might take up to 2 years just to build a healthy credit score - building credit is not an overnight thing. But it can certainly be done with patience and a lot of discipline.

PART 3:

LEVERAGING THE SYSTEM

This part of the book will focus on showing you the proper ways to leverage the credit system.

By this, I mean that my focus will be on showing the proper ways and means of using credit in a way that will ensure that you get along very well with the system without causing yourself much trouble.

The lack of knowledge of this kind leads to the many problems people have today with credit. People just don't know how to make use of credit safely.

That said, let's begin by discussing:

5 Credit Mistakes And How To Avoid Them

What are some of the mistakes that people routinely make when it comes to credit? And is there a way that you can avoid them?

You see, the mistakes that people make and that inevitably land them into trouble with the credit system are not very unique. They tend to be consistent across the board. Knowing about them will help you steer clear of the very problems they cause.

Some of the most common ones include:

1. *Borrowing more than you can afford*

This is one of the biggest problems out there. And certainly one of the hardest to combat.

It is easy to mistake credit as a blank check to go on a reckless spending spree, buying things you can't possibly afford.

This is what you need to keep in mind, always. The money you borrow isn't yours, and you have to pay it back – every cent of it.

Most people fall into this trap because of the amount of money approved when applying for credit.

Simply because you have $30,000 pre-approved on your credit card doesn't imply that you should spend anywhere near that amount.

Spending within your means should be a key guiding principle here.

And few people can determine *what spending within your means* denotes without preparing a written budget. A budget is one of the most important tools out there that can help you figure out how much you bring in in the form of income and how much you spend on every expenditure category.

The Millionaire Next Door came as a shock to many people when the famed Dr. Thomas J. Stanley revealed that only the most successful people in our society want to know how much they spend every year on every product or service category.

Yet, most of us are under the erroneous impression that successful people are frivolous and hardly ever disciplined financially.

Here's the bottom line: make sure you prepare a household budget before you go out to take any form of credit. Try and fit in possible monthly payments and get an idea of how much you can reasonably afford to borrow.

2. *Not being familiar with terms on your credit*

Let me ask you this: Would you head out to a store, purchase some new and complicated machinery, head out home, plug it into the power socket, and started pressing whatever button in sight, without even checking the manual?

I know I wouldn't. And I would bet you that no sane person alive would attempt such a thing. It's a ridiculous and grossly exaggerated scenario.

I bought a washing machine the other day. And I have to say; the product comes with a manual that takes the form of a booklet.

Yet, despite my familiarity with all kinds of machines, I found it necessary to check out a few basic instructions from this manual. I wasn't going to risk damaging a new and expensive product out of sheer ignorance and stupidity.

Yet, I don't know too many people who take matters nearly as seriously when taking out credit. Few people are interested in knowing exactly what terms and conditions govern their use of a lender's money.

Matters such as interest rates, dates of payment, penalties associated with late payments, and others easily escape many people's attention.

This is risking financial suicide. Failure to consider such important information could put you into a lot of trouble.

This tends to be the case, especially with a credit card that arrives in the mail. It also tends to be the case with credit cards that are offered by less reputable lenders.

Thus, you find that people easily are suckered in by credit cards that offer special "teaser rates" such as 0% APR, but which quickly adjust to 24% APR or more in a matter of weeks.

The problem here doesn't just lie with the lenders who offer these toxic products. It also has to do with the consumer who barely takes the time to read through the fine print to understand every aspect of the offer they are receiving.

Make it your business to know everything about every credit you take out.

3. *Falling behind on your payments*

Unless you have a perverted desire to worsen your ability to pay off your balance on a card (or any other type of debt), pay your bills as soon as possible.

Some lenders will not hesitate to add late fees if you happen to delay your payment by as little as a single day. Some will take that as an excuse to jerk up interest rates.

You do not want any of that.

Set up systems to remind you in advance of the most critical dates you should be making your payments.

Also, remember that late payments can be added to your credit report. If this happens, your credit score will suffer.

Also, other lenders may take that as a signal to jerk up their interest rates too. Yes, it's true; a slight negative change in your credit score can dampen the enthusiasm of even those creditors with who you happen to be on good terms, leading them to increase the rates they charge you.

4. *Stretching your limits*

It goes without saying: your credit utilization ratio should not go beyond 30%.

I will say it again, "Do not let the pre-approved credit limits give you a false sense of security regarding borrowing." It is critical to be frugal when borrowing.

Lenders will be watching your credit utilization ratio like a hawk.

The moment you exceed what they deem safe parameters, you will immediately join their list of customers who get charged high-interest rates and fees.

Avoid that ugly scenario by borrowing responsibly, and only when you need the money.

5. *Falling for making minimum payments*

This is a particularly dangerous mistake that, on the face of it, seems harmless. But few things will get you into much trouble quite in the way it does.

Let me ask you this, "Do you have any idea of how compound interest works?"

You no doubt do.

The idea is that interest is charged on the principal amount plus any interest earned from the previous period. The period can be annual or month-based.

Compound interest is one of the most potent forces in wealth-building. A relatively small sum can easily be grown into a small fortune by simply compounding interest.

To illustrate, a measly $1,000 invested at a paltry 10% annually will grow to a princely $17,499 given 30 years.

Now, this very force can work against you in the credit world. Interest payments can compound every month and grow into a large sum given enough time.

And this is basically what happens when you opt to make minimum payments on your monthly credit card bill. An interest rate is simply slapped on your balance every time you make the minimum payment and roll over the bill to the next month.

Consequently, your balance will keep increasing with each passing month.

Now, your creditor isn't opposed to this because the minimum payments make for regular income. Also, the amount you owe keeps increasing, all of which work in the creditors' favor.

However, for you, this is all bad news. It just makes it harder for you to clear your debt. It chains you to your problem perpetually.

Do yourself a favor and pay off your balance as fast as possible to avoid this trap.

Student Loans – The Nightmare Of Americans

The Center for Responsible Lending has established that America's current student debt load stands at $1.5 trillion.

Given that sheer volume alone, along with the fact that only 27% of those who graduate from higher education institutions work in industries that they majored in, it would be safe to term the student debt problem as an American nightmare.

Consider this fact: a four-year college education is estimated to set you back roughly $122,000 on average.

And while you contemplate that, it is estimated that the median student debt load for the average borrower who manages to make it to graduation is $30,000.

Thus, many adults today, and especially young adults - find themselves riddled with student debt that could easily take them years (if not decades) to pay off. And that is frustrating.

A problem like this could seriously destroy your credit and your life.

Watching a documentary the other day, I recall at one point hearing a young woman lament the fact that she won't be able to get married and have children in good time, especially with the kind of student debt that she has.

I sympathized with her plight.

Given the grave nature of the situation, you must learn:

How To Navigate And Avoid Student Loans

You see, there is no reason to rack up a huge amount of student loans and put yourself in a precarious financial situation later in life, especially if you can help it.

Please don't get me wrong. I am not in any way implying that you should shun college education altogether, as some pundits have suggested. Education is important, if not vital if you aspire to earn a decent income and live a comfortable lifestyle as an adult.

But, putting everything on the line such that you come out owing tens or perhaps hundreds of thousands of dollars is a shameful situation that needs to be put to an end.

Here are a few ways you can do that.

i. *Early savings*

If you are a parent (or soon-to-be parent), this advice is especially very valuable.

Start saving early for your kid's college.

Don't wait till tomorrow. Don't wait till next week. Start right now. Later, you'll be happy that you did.

If you are a young adult who hasn't joined college yet, the same rule applies.

Look, the odds are very good that you will have to go to college later in life. Most people in this world will. It's almost inevitable.

So, why not get prepared for it as soon as you can? Why wait?

If you live with your parents and aren't well-off, I recommend getting a job early. Then put aside most of your earnings in savings, especially since much of your living expenses are subsidized at this point.

Have a conversation with your parents about placing the money in an account that provides tax advantages for college savers, such as a 529b.

Sure, you might have to start small. But little progress, if given enough time, turns big.

Some people manage to save enough this way to pay for more than their colleagues. But many don't manage to accomplish that feat. Nevertheless, whatever amount you will have saved will go a long way in reducing the amount of debt you will need to pay.

ii. Comparison- shop college options

You don't have to aim your sights on just one college option. There are countless options to select from.

Options are ranging from private colleges to state-sponsored colleges, to in-state colleges, to out-of-state colleges, to community colleges, you name it. You have to give yourself as many options as possible.

A difference in selection between any of these colleges could save you tens of thousands of dollars. And that is not cheap money.

Now, you want to factor in the quality of education in your selection criteria. It does you no good to cheap out only to receive education or training that is mediocre at best.

Check the performance records. Interview several objective third parties on the reputation of colleges you are considering. Find out how many graduates have been gainfully employed. Collect as many facts as you possibly can before making your decision.

You might find that it's a lot cheaper and certainly a lot better to attend an in-state college than an expensive out-of-state institution. And the quality of education might be the same, if not better.

iii.Explore scholarships, grants, or crowdfunding

Scholarships and grants are essentially free money that you can use to subsidize your college tuition heavily.

This is especially true if you happen to be an academically inclined person who regularly gets good to excellent grades. Most scholarships are offered with needy but academically gifted students in mind. If you belong to that ilk, you might be in great luck.

To kick-start your research into scholarships and grants, the **Federal Student Aid**[5] website offers a nice place to start.

It is important to keep in mind that you probably won't secure a scholarship during your first year. It gets a little easier to get one in subsequent years. So, patience and persistence are key to getting one.

Just be sure to keep your grades up once you get one. Failure to maintain good academic performance while under a scholarship might be grounds for being kicked out of the program.

Further help can be obtained by seeking out crowdfunding sites such as **Kickstarter, Indiegogo,** and the like.

By telling a compelling story on sites like these, you can raise some money to subsidize further your tuition fees, books, and other college accessories.

---

5   https://studentaid.gov/understand-aid/types/scholarships

iv. Acquire knowledge on your potential income

Here's another thing you need to do: Research real-world professionals in your line of study. How much does the average person in your field make in a year?

This step will not increase the amount of money you use to reduce your college debt problem. It will accomplish something even more important. It will reduce the odds of you winding up with bad debt and struggling throughout your life.

The basic idea is this: if the annual cost of college tuition (and related expenses) is higher than the median annual salary of real-world professionals in your chosen field, then that is a sign that you should reevaluate your options.

Look at it this way: You don't want to be spending more on your education than you will likely make in the real world. It's completely ridiculous.

Most successful businesses would never consider taking out commercial loans if the upside in a venture was smaller than the downside risk of borrowing. You must have the same mentality.

Either choose a different course of study or select a different and cheaper college option.

v. Work while studying

Lastly, but not least, you can consider working part-time as you study.

Yes, I know what you are thinking. Nothing about it sounds sexy - especially if your line of study is demanding, like, say - law.

Well, at the risk of sounding trite, I will tell you this - what doesn't kill you makes you stronger. All that struggle will make you a tougher person who can deal with much adversity later in life.

I know because I did the same thing while trying to put myself through college, and it wasn't easy. Working and studying at the same time is one of the toughest combinations out there.

But, it can be done. There is nothing impossible about it.

Want to know what could be worse? How about graduating with a whopping $80,000 in student loan debt, as I have seen in some cases.

How would you like to start in life with that kind of pressure?

It's better to save your future self some trouble by helping solve part of the problem much earlier so that you can deal with a much smaller issue later on.

I hope these few tips will give you some great ideas on reducing or even eliminating the problem of student debt. It might shock you, but many people don't even bother to explore these very simple options.

But trust me when I tell you. They can serve you a great deal and put you in a much better position than you would be if you simply ignored them altogether.

The Good, Great, and Bad about Credit Cards

Data from Shift processing shows that 70% of Americans[6] own credit cards.

This should tell you something. Credit cards form an integral part of the credit system in our nation.

So doing without them is unthinkable.

And truth be told, there are some very useful purposes that credit cards serve that we simply can't turn a blind eye to.

But, credit cards also pose a catch-22 situation. If abused and wrongfully used, credit cards pose a serious threat to the financial lives of those who use them.

For that reason, we will spend some time exploring the good, the great, and the bad stuff involving credit cards.

The idea is to give you the knowledge you need never to overstep the boundaries and wreck your financial health.

So here we go.

What Are Credit Cards Good For?

We'll start with the good. Having a credit card will benefit you in the following ways:

1. *Cashless purchasing options*

In the digitized world that we live in today, who wants to carry around a bag of cash any time a big purchase

---

6   https://shiftprocessing.com/credit-card/

is around the corner? Do you think that the risk of getting robbed is worth it?

Me neither.

And that's all thanks to credit cards. All the money you have or need to access is carried around in that plastic card that can be tucked in your wallet.

And if you are shopping at the supermarket, and the new 50 inch curved-screen TV happens to catch your eye, all you need to do is take out your card and swipe.

This is a luxury we couldn't afford only a few decades ago.

2. *Ability to dispute charges*

This is another unique benefit that you will never get with cash – you can dispute and even reverse a fraudulent transaction.

Think of the implications of this. Have you ever worried about shopping for something online? Has it ever occurred to you that at some point, the seller could misrepresent facts about what they are selling? Has it ever worried you that you could one day become the victim of such manipulation?

Well, worry no more. Because you can always write to the credit card company and dispute a charge on the card, the credit card company would suspend that transaction and investigate the matter. If it turns out that the seller did not honor the terms of the agreement between the two of you, the transaction would never go through, and you would get your money back.

Think about it. How cool is that? This would be almost impossible to pull off if you were using cash.

3. *Ability to pay for things over time*

We all know about those potential high ticket purchases that involve money that we couldn't possibly afford right away.

Credit cards make it possible to buy something right now and pay for it later or slowly over time.

This is a convenience that means a lot to plenty of people. And to some extent, when used for the right purposes, it can be a life-saver.

Think of it this way. You are driving to work, and your car breaks down in the middle of nowhere. Now you have to call a mechanic to get some assistance in fixing it.

But there's a problem. It's the middle of the month, and you are low on cash reserves. And your mechanic will most certainly need to be paid.

What do you do?

In instances like these, a credit card comes in handy. You can just pay off the car repair fees right now with the expectation that you will pay back the money you owe sometime later down the road.

Wouldn't you love that?

4. *Ability to smooth out unstable cash flows*

Not everybody has predictable patterns of cash flow.

This is certainly true among many self-employed people or businesspeople. Short-term ups and downs in income tend to be the rule rather than the exception.

There are times when you can go for days, weeks, even months without receiving pay. This isn't in any way supposed to imply that your business or professional practice is failing. Many times, it is just a matter of annoying red-tape involving payments due.

In instances like this, having good credit is essential if you hope for a smoother ride in life. You can just borrow money to deal with business or living expenses and pay back the money once you get paid.

And since many lenders won't provide conventional loans for circumstances like these, having access to a credit card pretty much ends up doing it for you.

5. *Earning rewards*

Issuers of credit cards often provide various offers as incentives meant to draw prospects into doing business with them. In other cases, the offers are made available by merchants.

Often these offers take the form of:

- Air travel miles

- Discounts or gift cards

- Low introductory rates

- Insurance covers

- Cashback on purchases

These are partying gifts you could never get access to any other way.

6. *Building credit*

The best way to build credit is to take credit.

And that is what credit cards allow. If they are used responsibly, and payments are made on time, then using credit cards for a long period will generate a long credit history. And that will go a long way in improving your credit score.

The Pitfalls Involving Credit Cards

Okay, now that we've seen the upside of owning credit cards, how about we get familiar with the downsides as well.

i. Temptation to overspend

This is, without a doubt, the biggest reason why people get into trouble with credit.

Credit cards make it all too easy for people to stretch their means of livelihood to where paying back the money borrowed becomes a problem.

Credit cards give the false sense of having more money to spend than is available to the consumer.

This is even made worse by the fact that today we have become a consumption-oriented society. Spending heavily seems to be the norm.

And since most of us wish to emulate the habits of those around us, it is difficult for most people (even those with the strongest will) to fight back consumption tendencies.

Look at it this way: Imagine that you have a credit card that has been approved for a limit of up to $10,000. If you happen to live among people who earn high incomes and spend accordingly, what are the odds that you will hang out with them and fail to spend even a single cent from that card?

You know the answer.

ii. Reduction of future income

It helps to always keep in mind that using debt is all about spending tomorrow's income today.

And nowhere is that principle more evident than in credit cards. Every time you swipe that card, you may feel a little proud for having spent some money on something for the moment.

But in reality, what you are doing, is effectively ensuring that you will have less to spend tomorrow when you have to pay off that debt.

iii. High interest and fees

As a rule, the interest on credit cards is one of the highest out there.

After all, most credit cards are unsecured, forcing lenders to compensate for the risk of loss by increasing interest rates.

In some cases, the interest rates can be downright exploitative, especially if you do not deal with reputable high street lenders.

When interest rates are sky-high, you will struggle with your debt, and you will have to endure a great deal of stress in your life.

Another threat to your peace and financial security are the fees. Many lenders have fees that they levy upon borrowers, especially if certain conditions are violated.

These fees are so high; they interfere with your ability to pay down the debt promptly. Meanwhile, your income and your credit suffer as a result.

So be sure to check the **terms and conditions** paperwork that comes with every credit card before you decide to take the plunge. Be sure that everything that you discover is acceptable to you before you get involved.

iv. Dwindling credit

It is very likely that, unless you subscribe to a disciplined regimen regarding your use of credit cards, you will end up abusing them – just like most people do.

And when you commit classic credit card felonies such as exceeding your credit limit, failing to pay the balance on time, making minimum payments, applying for more credit cards, and so on, you will find that your credit will suffer as a result.

I needn't mention the trouble you can go through if your credit score ends on the lower end of the scale. You have trouble securing jobs, renting places to live, and getting more credit to happen to be some of the highlights.

v. Risk of fraud

It's also relatively easier for criminals to perpetrate credit card fraud.

For one thing, if someone steals your credit card, and you fail to report the matter as quickly as possible so that the card is canceled, then many will go on a ridiculous shopping spree that could turn your financial world upside down.

Another shocking truth is that fraud can be carried out on you if cybercriminals happen to break into databases that have stored credit card information.

You might reasonably assume that your lender has stable and secure systems that might make it difficult to compromise. But, can you say the same of the retailers, online shopping stores, and other merchants that you've given your credit card information to during purchases?

Well, realize that the hackers who are after this kind of data are not targeting the giants who likely have formidable security measures in place. They are after juicier targets that are more relaxed about matters regarding security. And often, systems run by these less enthusiastic third parties are full of security holes that could place financial data at risk.

No need to worry. If it turns out that your case was one of genuine fraud, the odds are good that your funds will be reimbursed.

Now that you are sufficiently knowledgeable about credit cards, see you in the next section where we talk about:

Preparing To Buy A House

Besides funding college, the purchase of a house is another instance that will likely involve major use of credit. In fact, for most people, purchasing a home will end up being their biggest financial commitment.

Given what is at stake, it is vital to know how you can navigate this process safely without posing a serious risk to yourself.

So, we will cover the most critical steps you will need to follow to handle home purchases in the most graceful way possible.

Let's jump right in.

Step 1: Taking a look at your budget

Regardless of what you might think, buying a home isn't for everyone. Many people are better off just renting.

If you have a low income and have trouble making ends meet, buying a home might be financial suicide.

Even if you happen to have a large income, but most of it gets spent on family and related expenses, owning a home might be riskier.

Why do I say that?

Because owning a home isn't just about paying the purchase price. Certain costs are all complements to being a homeowner.

Home repairs, property taxes, homeowner's insurance, private mortgage insurance, and home association fees (HOA) happen to top that list.

So, you need to look at your financial situation and weigh the merits and demerits of owning a home.

Here's where a budget comes in handy. Now, we'll cover budget-making later on, but at this point, understand that your budget is an important tool that will help you assess whether homeownership is the proper decision for you and your loved ones.

If your budget points to a lot of wiggle-room as well as savings, then you probably could afford a home that comes with a mortgage that is comparable to your monthly rent.

If it appears that you are barely keeping your head above water, then you should let this idea pass. Or wait until later when you are in a much healthier financial position.

Hint: *Your rent should not cost more than 30% of your monthly income if you wish to buy a home.*

Step 2: Looking at your savings

The next thing you do is take a look at your savings.

Do you have any? Most people don't

And if you do, is it enough to put down a deposit on a house?

Recall that a house will cost you on average $226,800 here in the U.S.

And in most cases, you might have to come up with anywhere between 10% and 20% of the value of your dream home for a bank or any other lender to agree on a mortgage deal.

That is some serious money that you might not have saved up. I am, of course, referring to savings upwards of $20,000. If you can't come up with that money fast (from your savings), you should probably wait until you can.

Step 3: Considering what you can afford

Given the money you have in savings, the wiggle-room in your budget, as well as your annual income, how much home can you afford?

That is a pertinent question. And definitely, one that needs answering.

Often, people mistake overstretching themselves and landing themselves in trouble when a little deliberation and careful thought would have served them better.

Now, there is much that has been said out there by pundits on the ways and means you should rely on when determining how much home you can afford.

I have my own preferred rule, which gets to the point and avoids complicated math. And it is so simple; anyone can rely on it.

The mortgage on your home should never cost more than twice your combined household income.

I give the late Dr. Thomas J. Stanley of **The Millionaire Next Door** (and other best-selling books) credit for this rule. Perhaps no one ever touted the concept of frugality and responsible spending quite in the manner he did.

Step 4: Considering the closing costs

It is also important to consider closing costs as part of the package.

As the name suggests, closing costs are the professional fees paid during the closing phase of a real estate transaction (in this case, a home purchase). They usually average 2% to 5% of the purchase price of the house.

Usually, closing costs can be negotiated between the parties involved. In some cases, the seller will agree to cover some of the costs, leaving the rest to the buyer.

In other cases, either the buyer or the seller takes responsibility for such costs.

But, I recommend being prepared beforehand to avoid surprises that could shock you into a state of panic. Factor in closing costs as part of your budget meant for purchasing a home. That is the only way to be sure.

I say this because closing cost negotiations can be dependent on the type of market you are participating in. In a sellers' market, for instance, you will probably never have the luxury of negotiation.

Step 5. Shopping for a mortgage

Shopping for a mortgage is necessary if you hope to get the best deal. And it should be done before you set out to carry out your house hunting.

This is a useful exercise because taking the time to secure a good mortgage should save you a couple of tens of thousands of dollars over the loan's life. At the beginning of this book, we saw how even a two-point differential could make a big difference. Always keep that in mind and take your time.

Now, on the topic of mortgages, there are a couple of things you need to know.

The first has to do with the type of mortgage. The two types of mortgages out there are fixed-interest as well as variable interest mortgages. The difference between the two is that with the former, interest paid remains the same throughout the loan's life. With the latter, the interest varies, depending on prevailing market conditions and interest rates.

I recommend that unsophisticated individuals opt for fixed-interest mortgages since they offer the much-needed predictability in payments. While variable-interest mortgages mean lower rates due to the added risk taken on, there's never telling what might happen in the future.

Perhaps that level of risk is meant for real estate professionals who can afford to keep a keen eye on interest rates during different market cycles. Ordinary consumers often have no such interests.

The second issue has to do with points. Points merely refer to prepaid interest on your mortgage.

Often, lenders offer borrowers the option between paying points and not paying any at all. The idea is that paying points allows you to save money by receiving a lower interest rate.

Now, in the years I have been in the business I am in, I have learned that paying points is only beneficial if you intend to keep your house for many years. Otherwise, you are better off just shunning the opportunity.

I urgently need to make an important point here. Before you get down to sign papers with a lender and provide details for them to do a credit check on you, make sure you have done your research and mean business. Recall that too many credit inquiries can lower your credit score – a situation you want to avoid as much as possible.

Step 6. Getting a pre-approval letter

Once a lender has done their homework on you and feels that you are a worthy proposition, you have to ask for an approval letter from them.

This is written proof that the lender is willing to extend credit of a certain amount should the deal go through.

This is important because having such a letter presents you as a serious buyer when making offers to sellers. And this means that you are more likely to win the bidding process if you run into a situation involving multiple buyers.

Step 7. Going ahead with the purchase

If everything works out as outlined in the previous steps, then you are ready to proceed with the rest of the transaction.

I recommend hiring an experienced real estate agent and an attorney to help you handle the rest of the purchase process.

A good real estate agent will help you find competent inspectors, appraisers, and even escrow agents. He/she will even help you with the negotiation process, which could lead to a better price on the deal.

On the other hand, the real estate will help handle the paperwork and look into legal matters regarding the property.

These professionals only get paid when a deal goes through, so they are usually committed to helping clients navigate the purchase process with as few glitches as possible.

And that, friend, is how you go through making a home purchase. Next up, we will look into how you can recuperate and rebuild your credit after going through some of the worst financial situations you could ever experience.

REBUILDING CREDIT AFTER FACING TROUBLE

There are certain difficult moments in life that can knock you out of balance and destroy your credit in the process.

The psychological pain associated with these moments is bad enough. But, if you ever hope to get your life back on track, it helps to know how you can rebuild your damaged credit as part of the recovery process.

In this chapter, that will be our main focus. In particular, we will be looking into bankruptcy, foreclosure, divorce, and repossession. Let's discuss each one of these situations in turn.

1. *Foreclosure*

As you well know, a foreclosure happens when you fall behind in your mortgage payments, so much so that your bank or mortgage lender is forced to take possession of your property to mitigate losses on their part.

And since foreclosures involve court proceedings, they are quickly made available as public records and find their way into your credit report. Once it is there, it stays for as long as seven years before it is expunged.

Now, it is important to note that foreclosures represent a serious breach of faith, at least from the lender's perspective. For this reason, foreclosures usually take a huge bite out of your credit score.

As a rule, the higher your credit score was, the heavier the hit.

FICO reports that someone with a credit rating that would be termed as "good" can expect to see as much as 100 points (perhaps more) knocked out of their score. If, on the other hand, your credit rating was "excellent," expect to see 160 points (or more) being deducted from your score.

So, foreclosures take the form of a double-bereavement. Not only do you lose your home, but you also lose your place among creditors' most revered client lists.

Nevertheless, foreclosures are never meant to imply that your life is over. If you take proactive steps, their impact on your score usually fades.

Okay, the first and most important thing you do is assess your situation and pinpoint the cause of your misfortune. This problem didn't just crop out of nowhere. It was caused by some mistake on your part.

You have to ask yourself:

- Is it possible that I spent beyond my means?

- Was my problem that of taking on too much debt?

- Could it be that I selected the wrong lender to work with? One who served me with a high-interest mortgage?

- Could it be that I wasn't keeping close track of my finances?

- Is owning a home even the right decision for me?

- Did you lose your job unexpectedly?

- Did you fail to set aside reserves for emergencies?

This is the time for serious introspection and honest answers. Once you have pinpointed the major causes of events that eventually precipitated your foreclosure, find solutions to them so that you never have to go through the same ordeal.

For instance, you can set a goal of preparing a household budget that helps control spending and keeps you out of trouble. Or you could opt to live in rental apartments that allow you the flexibility to downsize whenever the situation demands it.

Other steps you could take are generally applicable to everyone who wishes to rebuild credit. Such steps may include:

- Obtaining and making use of secured credit cards

- Making all your monthly bill payments in time

- Keeping an eye on your credit utilization ratio (never letting it go beyond 30%)

- Paying off balances on credit cards

- Check and clean up inconsistencies in your credit report

2. *Repossession*

Another potentially devastating episode in your life can involve repossession.

Repossession takes place with regards to vehicles that have been bought on credit. You see, if you buy a car with financing (which is what most people do), you are essentially taking a loan that requires monthly payments until the vehicle is paid for.

It is important to note that when you buy a car in this manner, the lender retains ownership of the vehicle title. This means, if you happen to default on payments or violate the terms stipulated when taking the loan, the lender can legally take possession of the car.

Your lender, of course, does this to recover their money. Your car will be sold off at an auction, and the money used to pay down your outstanding balance. In some cases, the vehicle may not sell for anywhere close to the amount owed, and the lender is forced to declare the remaining amount as a *deficiency balance*.

Having your car taken away from you is not a pretty thing to go through. But even more disturbing is the fact that the repossession shows up in your credit report. And, just as it is with the case of foreclosures, repossessions remain in your report for seven years.

Okay, if you are reading this and have already lost your car to repossession but wish to rebuild your credit, then the rules of rebuilding credit previously discussed apply.

But, if you are teetering on the brink but haven't lost your car yet, you might find the following suggestions useful:

i. Contact your lender and negotiate

The moment you realize that there's an impending problem regarding you paying your car loan as agreed, it's time to place a call to your lender or pay them a visit in person.

Then, if you make your case properly, chances are the two of you might work out a deal that works out for both of you.

First, you have to work out whether your issue is a temporary one. Perhaps you've hit a stumbling block that is making things a bit harder for you right now. Perhaps you are confident that your situation will change in a short while and that you will fulfill your obligations.

In such a case, your lender may agree to a deferment. This is an arrangement that allows you to go for a few months without making loan payments, with the understanding that the amount you owe (along with interest) still stands.

Another possibility is that your lender may agree to a new payment plan. In this scenario, your lender simply agrees to craft a new plan for paying the remainder of your loan (which may include more lenient terms). This option may be considered if you have demonstrated trustworthiness in making previous payments on time.

ii. Sell the vehicle

This is another viable option worth pursuing.

If it has become clear to you that coming up with payments will be a major issue, don't wait until the situation worsens. Simply unload your car.

After selling the car, you could come up with enough money to pay off all your debt and perhaps have some leftover for a cheaper car.

The benefits associated with exercising this option are twofold. First, you save yourself the pain and humiliation of going through the drama that typifies repossession. You get to handle the situation in a manner that is more dignifying to you.

Second, your car may sell for a lot more than if your lender was to have it sold at an auction. Generally, items at auctions are sold off at much lower prices because they often attempt to recover money lost and not turn a profit.

So, if you take matters into your own hands, you may come up with money that can more than cover your balance with the lender.

iii.Refinance your debt.

If your credit history shows good behavior, you may be able to get the lender to agree to a refinancing deal.

In this instance, your lender may agree to charge you a lower interest and extend the loan term to give you more breathing room.

iv. Surrender the car voluntarily

Now, this option may not be that good since its impact on your credit history is nearly the same as that of a repo.

But, it allows you to keep your dignity intact. And, in a way, you may get the lender to show you a little mercy later on.

It also costs you less money because the services of a tow truck are usually imposed on you.

The basic idea here (if you haven't realized it already) is that handling the situation in your way is a lot better than letting nature take its course and having to deal with the consequences of a repo record in your credit report.

BANKRUPTCY

Now we get to talking about bankruptcy.

It's a legal process that involves people or businesses that have failed to meet their debt obligations. As such, you (or a business entity) can seek protection and relief from creditors.

It usually involves making your case before a court of law and proving that your income, as well as assets, are far too little to guarantee payment of debts.

The idea is that you will either be given more time to address your financial situation and pay back the debts you owe or have them completely written off.

And that brings us to the two types of bankruptcies that exist – Chapter 7 and Chapter 13.

Chapter 7

Most people who file for bankruptcy usually opt to take this option.

It works like this: The court cross-examines you and determines that your income is far too low to pay your debts reasonably.

When the court determines this, the solution usually becomes one of selling whatever little assets you may have so that some money is raised to pay off your creditors.

So essentially, your home, car, or any other item in your possession that is reasonably liquid will likely be taken away from you and sold off at an auction.

Now, the court has discretion power in this decision. That is, it usually looks at your situation to determine what can be sold and what can be kept.

After the money has been paid off to creditors, whatever balance is left is usually charged off by the court. So essentially, you get a clean slate.

But the clean slate usually comes at a cost, though. The first and most obvious cost has to do with your credit. According to FICO, a bankruptcy of this kind can make a *"good"* credit score fall off the cliff by 200 points.

Second, this type of bankruptcy goes into your credit report and stays there for a solid ten years.

Chapter 13

Chapter 13 bankruptcy takes on a different form.

Here, after the court has looked at your case, it may determine that you are going through a rough patch that is likely to get better with time.

Therefore, instead of auctioning off your assets, the court decides to "buy you some time" so that you can sort out your issues.

This means that your debts don't get written off. The terms are simply adjusted to allow for more flexibility and breathing room.

Specifically, the court works with you to develop a sensible monthly payment plan unique to your situation. This may stretch the time you need to pay off your debts by as much as 3 to 5 years.

You also get to work with a budget that the court monitors itself until your problem gets solved.

It is worth noting that this type of bankruptcy will not have as much impact on your credit as its counterpart. Unlike Chapter 7, this type of bankruptcy will remain on your credit report for seven years. Your score will also not take such a big hit. You will likely shed off anywhere from 130 to 150 points.

But there's something you have to keep in mind. Even though both of these bankruptcy codes work well to offer you a reasonable amount of protection, they typically don't forgive you from the following:

- Unpaid student debt

- Tax liens, penalties, and fines

- Child support and alimony

Okay, so how do rise above the mire of bankruptcy? As I've stated before, there are no magic solutions. You simply have to follow classic credit-building techniques that we've covered previously and have a lot of patience because you will need it.

Divorce

Lastly, we talk about divorce.

You were in love with someone. And you are no longer in love. Everything you had has come to an end.

You are not alone. And it doesn't mean that there's something necessarily wrong with you. It has often been said that slightly more than 1 in 2 marriages ends in divorce.

When you think about such odds, it's easy to see that you are more likely to get divorced than to end up in a car accident.

But here's the real issue with divorce: Not only is it hurtful to your emotions, but it is also injurious to your finances.

Lawyer fees are usually through the roof, to begin with. And suppose you are a man who was the main breadwinner but who didn't have the foresight to sign a prenuptial agreement. In that case, you are easily looking at the surrender of fifty percent of your assets, and that does not even include alimony and child support payments.

Divorce also affects your credit, but not in the manner bankruptcies, foreclosures, or repossessions do. The effect is somewhat indirect.

First of all, consider the fact that most divorces occur due to financial conflict. And such conflicts usually center on credit issues. So right off the bat, divorces end with debt problems of some sort that reflect in credit reports.

Secondly, divorce affects joint ownership of accounts. According to **Experian**, the very act of splitting up joint accounts usually changes your credit history, which consequently harms your score.

So, what can you do to alleviate the consequences of divorce on credit?

Aside from the obvious ones that we've discussed, there are two main ones I can come up with. They are:

1. *Opening up your accounts*

If you are in a position to get lenders to pay attention to you and lend you money at reasonable interest rates, then open up accounts with them, albeit in your name.

This is a good move in the right direction because it allows you to build credit in your name, which will be a better reflection of your habits concerning credit.

Over time, your credit will benefit because of it.

2. *Removing yourself as an authorized user*

Recall how I mentioned earlier about an authorized user being on the hook for bad credit behavior perpetrated by the person they choose to trust? Well, nowhere is that point exemplified than in a situation involving divorce.

You see, there's no way for you to keep tabs on your ex's credit behavior. For all you know, the hard times they go through could lead them to spiral into debt problems easily. You want to take yourself out of the picture before you end up paying for their sins.

3. *Close joint accounts*

This may end up being the main cause of problems with your credit. Remember that closing accounts usually affect your credit utilization ratio.

But it is better done as soon as possible so that you can begin building your credit without any encumbrances.

Leaving such accounts open leaves you at the mercy of your ex-spouse's bad financial habits – a situation you want to avoid at all costs.

In a nutshell, if you ever find yourself in any one of these compromising situations, just keep in mind that all is not lost. With a little effort to work the fundamentals and exert patience on your part; eventually, the grass will grow again.

PROTECTING YOURSELF FROM IDENTITY THEFT

In this chapter, we will talk about a very sensitive matter – identity theft. It is arguably one of the most popular crimes in the United States today. The Federal Trade Commission (FTC) says that it receives more reports of crimes of this nature than any other consumer complaint.

So...

What Is Identity Theft Anyway?

Identity theft is a crime that involves one person using personally identifiable information belonging to another person to masquerade as that person.

Personal identifiable information (PII) simply refers to any piece of data that could be used to identify a person. Examples of personally identifiable information include:

- Your social security number

- Your full name

- Your driver's license number

- Your bank account number

- Your credit card number, along with its card verification code (CVC)

- Your email

- Your passport number

- Your physical address

The weakness of how our systems have been set up is that anyone can show up at a financial institution and provide information such as the one above. He or she would be treated as that person regardless of whether they were the person they claimed to be.

Rarely is visual confirmation ever needed when providing this kind of information. This allows criminals to slip undetected and assume other people's identities.

Stolen identity information can be used in all manner of ways. But chief among them is financial. Yes, someone can assume your identity to apply for credit and use it.

This flaw allows a criminal to go on a shopping spree, clean out bank accounts, take vacations at exotic places, and do just about everything imaginable under the sun that money can do.

And guess who picks up the tab for all that? You do.

This is as serious as identity theft gets. And the worst part about it is that it happens often, and there are no easy solutions in sight.

Now...

How Can You Tell That You Are A Victim Of Identity Theft?

The worst part about identity theft is that it is hard to detect it very quickly. Much of the time, it can occur without your knowledge until something outrageous happens that brings it to your attention.

So, much of the time, the damage is already done before discovering what is going on.

Nevertheless, here are some warning signs you should watch out for.

1. *Unexplained records on your bank statement*

You can determine that you are under the threat of identity theft if you request your bank account statement and see unfamiliar transactions.

Look through the transaction history - do you see any withdrawals that you did not authorize yourself?

2. *There are unexplained transactions in your credit card statement*

Besides bank statements, you should review credit card statements regularly.

The moment you spot an unfamiliar record, you should be wary and investigate further.

3. *Your bills are missing, or they look suspicious.*

In case a criminal changes your home address to hijack your mail, you may find that your bills don't arrive when they should.

If they happen to arrive, you may get bills that are inconsistent with what you are used to paying.

4. *Receiving strange calls from debt collectors*

You know you have behaved well with regards to your credit, and then, bam! You receive an angry call from a collector who is desperately asking you to pay back the money you owe.

Any report that reflects unknown behavior on your part should raise eyebrows. Other signs include the following:

- A medical bill that you are unaware of

- Inability to file taxes (someone else has filed them for you)

- A warrant for your arrest on crimes you did not commit

- You've applied for credit, and your application has been declined.

What Should You Do When You Suspect Your Identity Is Stolen?

The good thing is that identity theft is so common that there are measures and protocols to handle possible cases. Therefore, you likely won't run into frustration if you suggest to relevant parties that you may be a victim of identity theft.

Now here are several things that you do once you become suspicious.

1. *Contact your creditor*

If your credit card was stolen, and it's clear to you that someone is using it to make purchases, contact your credit card company immediately.

Request them to cancel your card as soon as possible. Denying the criminal any more access to your account is one of the surest remedies to this kind of problem.

2. *Contact the credit bureaus*

Another thing you do is contact the credit bureaus as soon as possible and explain your situation.

Such action will prompt them to freeze all your credit information. Also, they put out an alert to all your creditors, who may then close out accounts that haven't been affected yet. This should take place within 24 hours after you have reported the problem.

You may also get the privilege of issuing a victim statement so that anyone who requests to see your credit reports is made aware of your situation and that the data is completely unreliable.

After you do this, each of the three credit bureaus should send you copies of your credit reports, which you should file away safely.

3. *Notify law enforcement*

You also need to make sure you notify the police. They may not take part in actively investigating the matter or resolving it in any way. But filing a report with them helps bolster the credibility of your claim.

For instance, if a lender is having trouble believing your story, you can send them a copy of the police report to show them that you are telling the truth.

4. *Notify the FTC*

Notifying the FTC will also benefit you in proving your case.

Sure, they will not take the matter into their own hands. They are usually involved in keeping records and analyzing the data to establish patterns. But having them on your side will certainly make you more believable.

5. *Notify your post office*

At times, identity theft crimes are perpetrated through the mail. And in some instances, the issue involves some form of unauthorized access to user data at the post office. So bringing the matter to their attention may certainly prompt better security measures or internal investigations.

Steps To Reduce the Probability Of Identity Theft

Fighting identity theft is a matter of reducing the chances that you will become a victim. The fact is, criminals in this space are always devising new tactics to access people's data. There's no telling what their next best move will be.

However, here are some basic practices that might keep you on the safer side of things:

1. *Carry out transactions online*

We live in a digitized world where everything is being digitized. And that includes financial transactions.

Therefore, it means that you can handle important requests and financial transactions online, instead of the old and less secure mail that can easily be intercepted or broken into.

If, for instance, you need to gain access to your banking statements, you can simply log onto your bank's portal and download reports for whatever period you desire. And the beauty about downloading reports this way is that you can access them anytime you need them, which makes it all the more likely that you will spot inconsistencies faster.

2. *Beware of phishing*

Phishing is a tactic used by cybercriminals to trick users into giving up valuable information. You know - such as personally identifiable information

Phishing works this way: a criminal crafts a credible-looking web page claiming to be a popular service vendor, such as an online bank. Then, the link to the web page gets sent to an unsuspecting victim via email.

The email is usually professionally written and convincing. For instance, the email may request the reader to provide their details for verification or security purposes.

The object is to get the reader to click on the link, head over to the fake web page, and give up their personal information (such as bank account number, credit card number, pin, name, and so on), thinking that they are carrying out a legitimate request.

Preventing phishing is quite simple. Simply check the address bar on the browser to see if the URL resembles that of the service provider in question. You see, ordinary cybercriminals can never get access to your service provider's actual website address (unless they are very sophisticated hackers who manage to gain access to the main server).

Also, it must start with https:// instead of http:/. The latter is a less secure protocol and is never used to transport sensitive data over the internet.

Also, most service providers inform clients and customers that they never request personal information through the mail.

3. *Keep the data on your computer secure*

While you transact highly confidential material through your computer, you must make sure that the computer's security and the data in it are not compromised.

If the computer is stolen or highly sophisticated criminals manage to break into it remotely, then your private data will most certainly be exposed.

So here are some things that you might consider doing to prevent the likelihood of that happening:

- Protect access to your computer with a password. And don't make it obvious.

- Never leave your computer unlocked and unattended

- Ensure that you install antivirus software to prevent malicious programs from taking over your computer and stealing data from it.

- Never maintain a physical list of passwords and keep it close to your computer

- Before you get rid of your computer, be sure to delete all confidential information from it.

- Never share your password with anyone.

4. *Arrange for freezing of your credit reports*

You will realize that practically anyone who pretends to be you can run a credit check on you and learn where you stand.

So it may help to have some sort of protection scheme designed to protect your credit information. All three credit bureaus allow you to apply a credit freeze on your credit information, for free, upon request.

Essentially, this means that every time someone wishes to request a report of yours, you have to provide a PIN to authorize the request.

This prevents prying eyes from taking a peek at your information without your consent.

5. *Implement a fraud alert*

A fraud alert is supposed to prevent unauthorized account opening by identity theft criminals.

So, every time someone tries to open an account in your name, the fraud alert prompts the account opener to confirm their identity.

Just like with the credit freeze, you can request this feature from each of the three credit bureaus and at no cost whatsoever.

But, unlike the credit freeze, which can stay in place perpetually, a fraud alert stays active for a limited period (between 90 days and seven years)

6. *Be wary of sharing your social security number*

Your social security number is one of the key pieces of identity information that criminals could use against you.

So you want to be extremely careful about who you share it with. Only share it with trusted parties and organizations.

Besides, you want to be careful about how you mention it, especially in public spaces where people can overhear you. Often, it just takes a keen mind to take down that kind of information simply because you weren't discrete about it.

7. *Pick up checks in person*

A typical check contains your banking routing number along with your checking account number.

This information alone is usually to help criminals create a new check, making it possible to purchase items with your money.

The solution? Head over to the bank yourself and pick up your checks from there. Never agree to have them mailed over. Doing so will only open you up to unnecessary risk.

8. *Unsubscribe from pre-approved credit card offers*

You know those credit card offers that come in through the mail?

The paperwork comes with some personal identifiable information. Criminals can use that information against you by requesting cards in your name.

So, what do you do?

Simply shred those letters before you send them over to the trash can. You don't want those criminals ever making any use f that paperwork.

Alternatively, you can simply choose to unsubscribe from receiving those offers altogether. Knowing the dangers associated with applying for new lines of credit, you just don't need them.

BONUS CHAPTER
5 TIPS HOW TO SAVE MONEY

I saved this chapter for last because I believe that perhaps nothing will save your financial life more than being more deliberate with how you spend money.

Today, most people spend without giving much thought to how difficult it is to earn money. I tend to think that majority of the problems we currently have in our business and personal lives can be solved once we adopt frugal spending and saving habits.

That said, here at some tips to follow to accomplish that:

Tip 1: Budgeting

Do you sometimes feel like you don't know where all this money you make is always going? Like, the moment it hits your checking account, it is gone within a matter of days and disappeared, without a trace?

You are not alone. Most people feel the same way too.

So what is the answer to this age-old predicament? One word – budget.

I am often reminded of a quote by Dave Ramsey that goes like this:

"A budget is telling your money where to go instead of wondering where it went."

If you want to tame the magic that is usually involved in money, and gain some control over your life, prepare a budget right away.

Most people equate budgeting to living like an impoverished monk. Budgeting is perceived as something only people with low incomes need.

This attitude comes from the perceived restrictiveness of the practice, which many people resent. But it doesn't have to be that way. A budget doesn't have to be restrictive for it to be effective.

Budgeting is about allocating earned dollars in a way that will maximize your efficiency. No matter how much income you make, budgeting can help you maximize the utility of your earned income. When you look at it that way, budgeting can increase satisfaction with life.

That, said there are a few basic steps to creating a budget. And here they are:

Step 1: Assemble all your financial paperwork

Collect every financial document at your disposal that dates back to the past three months. Everything that will give an indication of income earned as well as money spent.

Here is a sample list of what you should be looking for:

- W-2 forms
- Paystubs
- Bank statements
- Credit card bills
- Investment accounts
- 1099s
- Utility bills
- Mortgage statements
- Auto loan statements
- Receipts

Step 2: Establish your monthly income

Start by looking at documents representing money that is brought in. Simply add up the amounts listed and divide the amount you determine by 3. This is an effort to determine your average monthly income, especially since, for some people, the amount earned each month can be variable.

Step 3: Determine your monthly expenses

You want to do the same thing as the previous step, only this time you will be looking at money that is going out.

Step 4: Separate the fixed from the variable expenses

To establish some form of order, you want to separate fixed expenses from variable ones. Fixed expenses stay the same throughout the entire period and are expected to stay that way. You can assign specific values to such items.

Variable expenses tend to go up and down. Here determining the average and assigning it to each item might prove useful.

Step 5: Total up your income as well as expenses

At this point, you want to create two columns on a piece of paper or spreadsheet. On each column, I want you to create an itemized list of your expenses and your income.

Then, total up the values in each one of them.

You should establish a certain truth at this point. If the difference between your income and your expenses is negative, you are spending beyond your means and need to find ways to cut back.

On the other hand, if the difference is positive, you are probably on the right track but could still use some tips on increasing your savings.

Step 6: Modify your expenses

If you are in a situation where your expenses outsize your income, you need to look for areas to cut back on spending.

Perhaps you could cut back on the amount spent dining out, on groceries, beer, and so on.

The idea is, if you have savings listed as an expense, you should at least aim to have both columns balance each other. If you haven't done so, then at the very least, the difference between your income and expenses should be big enough to meet your desired savings goal.

If you have followed these steps, you should have a budget you can work with. Alternatively, you could opt to head online and seek some pre-designed excel templates for budgeting.

Tip 2: Emergency savings account

While a budget is very useful in keeping your finances in good shape, it isn't everything.

Unforeseen events happen in life, and many of them require you to use the money to do something about them. These are unexpected expenses that your budget usually doesn't cover.

For example, what are you supposed to do when faced with any (or a combination) of these situations:

- You suddenly lose your job

- Your car suddenly breaks down and urgently needs repairs

- A medical emergency that isn't covered by insurance occurs

- There is an unexpected repair at your place of residence

- A member of your family has suddenly passed away, and you need to spend some money for the funeral

- A member of your family has gotten seriously ill, and you need to take some time off to provide some care

Having some money set aside to help out during any unfortunate situation can be a lifesaver. It will save you from enduring a great deal of stress or having to plunge into debt.

So, what amount should you set aside for your emergency fund?

It used to be thought that $1000 was adequate to fit this role. And it is certainly a lot better than having none at all. But the truth is, no rule is set in stone for this.

It all depends on your lifestyle, your occupation, your income, and all manner of factors.

But there a few rules you could follow and be on a safer side:

- Dave Ramsey has always advocated setting aside between 3 months' (for employed) and six months' (for the unemployed) worth of expenses. Your budget should give you a good estimate of what your expenses look like.

- Suze Orman has always advocated that people strive to set aside up to eight months' worth of expenses to be truly safe.

Both approaches work. If you are risk-seeking about life, then Dave Ramsey's rule would certainly be a better fit. But if you have a strong aversion to unexpected risks, then Suze Orman's approach will appeal to you better.

Now the question becomes one of where the money should be put. After all, this is money you want to have the freedom to have access to whenever a need arises without paying a hefty penalty.

I recommend putting it in either a money market account or a high yield savings account. Both of these accounts have served people so well over the years.

Tip 3: Follow the 50/30/20 rule

Nailing down a budget can be a herculean task. It usually involves making countless considerations and tradeoffs, none of which come easy.

Therefore, it helps to have a set of rules that can guide the decision-making process.

One of those rules is the 50/30/20 rule designed by Elizabeth Warren, who extensively covered the rule in her ubiquitous book, "All Your Worth: The Ultimate Lifetime Money Plan."

According to this rule, a properly designed budget should have roughly 50% of your net income going into your basic needs such as shelter, food, clothing, and medical expenses.

Then, an estimated 30% should go into providing for your wants. You know: things like dinner at fancy restaurants, vacationing in Paris, the new curved screen TV, the laptop computer, and so on.

Lastly, an estimated 20% should cater to your savings and investments plan. This is the money you get to stash away into retirement funds, emergency savings accounts, mutual funds, and so on.

The beauty of this rule is that it is all-rounded. It provides a much-needed balance in life. It allows you to meet your basic obligations, enjoy the good things, and still provide room for accomplishing important financial goals.

Tip 4: Follow the 30-day rule

There is yet another rule that you could follow and that can help you curb excessive spending.

You see, often, we purchase things that we don't need, and often on impulse. Most purchases are centered on gratifying emotional needs. Once the euphoria wears out, you are suddenly left with something that you never really needed, but that has punched a hole in your pocket.

What if you could end this cycle and keep most of your money instead?

That is what the 30-day rule helps you accomplish.

It's simple, and it works like this. Anytime you are faced with a burning desire to purchase something that is not an immediate need, restrain yourself. Take note of the item at the back of your mind and wait for 30 days.

If, at the end of 30 days, you find that you still have the object in your mind, much less need it, go and buy it. Otherwise, you are better off keeping your money and forgetting about it.

This rule works so well that people find that they have even forgotten about the object of their desire much of the time. And that leads to more savings.

Tip 5: Cook your meals at home

This is another important tip that could save you a lot of money.

Eating at restaurants every day is an expensive undertaking. You are essentially hiring someone else to do the cooking for you. So, they charge you more than you would if you had prepared the meal yourself. It's amazing how much money can be saved when you learn to prepare most restaurant meals at home.

This isn't to say that you shouldn't eat out at all. The occasional dinner at your favorite restaurant is perfectly fine as long as you have other financial goals met. But such a want should not be fulfilled every day since it is brutally expensive.

And here's another tip for when you order meals at restaurants – stay away from beverages and meat-based meals. Restaurants make a killing out of these two categories. And guess at whose expense? Yours, of course. Instead, order water or vegetarian dishes.

I hope you can learn to use these five simple but powerful tips for what they are good for. They can transform your financial life in ways you never deemed possible.

Q &A SECTION

I 've said before that I often have people coming to me with various questions about credit. Some of them have no doubt been answered by the material in this program.

But there remain others that are worth answering. Let's get to cover some of them.

Question:

How often can I expect my credit score to change?

Answer:

Well, it depends on the level of activity in your credit file.

Remember how I talked about the fact that factors such as debt payments, changes in the account balance, new hard inquiries, as well as changes to your outstanding debt can affect your credit?

The more often these events occur, the more frequently your credit file will be updated, and therefore, the more frequently your score will change. All it takes is for the computer to recalculate your score every time a change occurs to your file.

This can mean changes by the minute, by the hour, by the day, by the week, you get the idea.

Question:

Why do I often see many different credit scores?

Answer:

This is a particularly common issue among those who have no real grasp of the different scoring models that are out there.

So here's the deal: Apart from the scoring models we've just looked at, other models are industry-specific. That means you could easily find FICO and Vantage models for the auto industry, the mortgage industry, the insurance sector, and so on.

Now multiply all those different models across all the three major credit reference bureaus. Now you are looking at quite a number of them.

And here's another interesting part, banking and other credit firms are also beginning to create and implement their proprietary models to work with. So, you could easily be looking at so many different permutations of scoring models; they could easily boggle your mind.

Question:

When should I consider seeking the services of a credit counselor?

Answers:

Credit counseling can be a useful service for you if you are in a dire financial situation that requires a professional's services.

Typically, if you are in serious debt problems and are unsure whether to consider filing for bankruptcy or subscribing to a debt repayment program, credit counseling is for you.

A credit counselor will listen to your situation and offer professional advice on which course of action is most appropriate. A credit counselor is equipped to help negotiate interest rates and waivers from creditors on your behalf in many instances.

Now, there is one caveat to be aware of. Some agencies are debt collection agencies masquerading as credit counseling service providers. Their job is to simply put you into a debt management program and get kickbacks from creditors in the process.

It's big business. And this conflict of interest makes them particularly ill-equipped to provide objective advice to seekers of their services. You should stay away from these types of agencies.

One way to distinguish a genuine credit counseling agency from a so-called debt collector is to inquire whether they put you on a debt management program. A genuine credit counselor should not suggest that option right off the bat.

Question:

What is debt consolidation, and how does it help me?

Answer:

Debt consolidation is a way of combining all your debt obligations into one.

Let's say you have debt with many different lenders. And it is getting exhausting to track and manage payments to all of them. You can seek a debt consolidation loan from a lender such as a bank. This type of loan allows you to pay off all your creditors in full.

After that, you are only responsible for servicing one debt – the one offered to you by the bank.

You can think of it as a way of reducing the number of masters you serve and ending up with just one.

It might or might not be a good option, depending on the attractiveness of the offer provided by the provider of the debt consolidation loan.

Question:

Is there anything I can't dispute on my credit report?

Answer:

The short answer is no.

Credit reporting agencies are open to (and encourage) you to dispute inaccurate information in your reports.

And since every request is deeply investigated before any change is made, there's no real reason why the credit referencing bureaus would be opposed to this idea.

Question:

I make good money and pay my bills in good time. Why then are my credit scores so bad.

Answer:

First of all, kudos for being so responsible with your bills. Not everybody is that wise.

But, paying bills is not enough.

If you want to up your score in the credit system, you have to use it. There's just no way around it.

The system only works by the data that is fed to it. If there is little or no data at all, you will have poor scores or no scores. And that, my friend, will not make you attractive to creditors.

So, how do you solve this problem?

Take out some credit. Take out credit designed to help you build credit (Refer back to our discussion on building credit). Or become an authorized user.

You don't even have to use it, since that would be wastefulness. You can just sit on it and pay it back (with some interest, of course).

The more acquainted you become with the credit system, the better you will do.

Question:

How many credit cards should one have? And what is the ideal usage on those cards?

Answer:

First of all, the idea that having more credit cards somehow ups your value in the credit system should be forgotten immediately.

I recommend having as few cards as possible. The typical millionaires interviewed by Dr. Stanley throughout his career had two credit cards – one for business and one for personal use. I see no reason why you should go beyond that number.

I have mentioned before that if you have many cards already, keeping them open is smart. This advice applies only to those who have made the mistake of acquiring more credit cards than they need.

When you start, acquiring as few credit cards as possible is the smart move, not doing the opposite.

Question:

Are medical, and utility bills factored into my credit? How do they affect it?

Answer:

The answer to the first part of your question is that they aren't.

However, Experian has a product that allows you to import your utility bill payment history to be added to the system that calculates your credit score.

But, this service is exclusive to Experian, and it only involves utility bills. Medical bills are not part of it.

But, here's the interesting fact you need to know: failure to pay either of these bills on time, perhaps even for a long period, will most certainly result in a negative record in your credit reports, which will drive down your scores.

CONCLUSION

We've arrived at the end of our little journey together.

But before we wrap things up, I'd like to take some time to talk about the kind of work we do here at Depina Credit Solutions and the process that underlies it.

If you happen to take an interest in our services, here's a brief rundown of what we will do for you:

Step 1: Credit review

The first thing we will do, once we take you in as a client, is to conduct a credit check on you. We will conduct a comprehensive review of all your credit reports.

The object here will be to understand the nature of your financial health as quickly as humanly possible.

Once that is determined, we will suggest a plan of action that draws upon our collective experience in the business of helping people get out of shaky situations.

Step 2: Credit repair

After determining the nature of your credit, we will work with you to improve your situation.

Much of this work will involve what we have talked about in this program. The difference is, instead of going at it alone, you will be working with experienced professionals who have mastered every little nuance in the credit repair business.

So, in addition to rendering our considerable expertise, we will be leveraging their existing connections in the credit world to push through red tapes and pull favors on your behalf.

Step 3: Credit building

Lastly, once we've fixed the existing cracks in your credit, we will hold you by the hand in building your credit up so that you reach your highest potential.

Among other things, we will provide you with credit counseling services and the right education to keep you going and doing things in the right way.

After you have pulled yourself out of a hole, the last thing you want is to do things that will throw you back in. We do everything in our power to prevent that scenario by even providing one-on-one coaching to our most valuable clients.

If you feel as we do, that our services are a reasonable proposition, then feel free to reach us through:

- Our website – www.depinacreditsolutions.com

- Our email – info@depinacreditsolutions.com

- Our Telephone – (508) 9557171

It is my sincere hope that you have derived value from spending time with me in this program. You now know to get out there and battle at the frontlines in the world of credit, knowing for sure that no one will take advantage of your naiveté.

I thank you for your support in enrolling in this program, and may you be blessed abundantly.

CPSIA information can be obtained
at www.ICGtesting.com
Printed in the USA
BVHW011029220321
602886BV00020B/878